TREES AND PROTECTION OF ENVIRONMENT

TREES AND PROTECTION OF ENVIRONMENT

V.K. SHARMA
Former Professor of Horticulture,
Consultant (Horticulture),
Technical Coordinator (Apple)
Agricultural and Processed Food,
Products Export Development Authority (APEDA)

DEEP & DEEP PUBLICATIONS PVT. LTD.
F-159, Rajouri Garden, New Delhi-110027

TREES AND PROTECTION OF ENVIRONMENT

ISBN 81-7629-578-7

Typeset by ASHISH TECHNOGRAPHICS,
3190, Mohindra Park, Shakur Basti, Delhi-110034.

Printed in India at MAYUR ENTERPRISES,
WZ Plot No. 3, Gujjar Market, Tihar Village, New Delhi-110018.

Published by DEEP & DEEP PUBLICATIONS PVT. LTD.,
F-159, Rajouri Garden, New Delhi-110027.
Phones: 25435369, 25440916
E-mail: ddpbooks@yahoo.co.in • deep98@del3.vsnl.net.in
Showroom:
2/13, Ansari Road, Daryaganj, New Delhi-110002 • Telefax: 23245122

Dedicated to

ADITYA and **ABHINAV**

for their Love and Affection

CONTENTS

PREFACE

Environment protection and development have to go at a pace that is not harmful to the human beings. In fact, no development is possible without disturbing the environment. Roads being built to bring economic, social and cultural development in the surrounding areas, is a process in which the upper strata of the soil/earth is disturbed. During this process, trees, bushes and other flora specie are uprooted, much of the soil, stones and like material is removed from one place and shifted to another place leading to infertility at places where such material is being dumped either by nature or man. Without roads, no development is possible. Similar is the case while establishing big or small industries.

Industries are planned for bettering the economic conditions of the local people by providing employment, better living conditions and better economic returns to the people. It is another cause of concern that the benefits derived by establishing the industries are maximum for the big bosses or those who have invested large sums of money to establish rather than those who have actually worked for the establishment. During the establishment of such industries, pollution in air, soil, water and culture takes place. By emission of gasses and liquids, air, earth and water in the adjoining areas are polluted, and by the noise through working on machines and other heavy equipment. Such things also do happen when hydel projects are being established. One can name any industry and the impact of that industry on environment is there.

Trees have been serving the mankind since ages. They provide us the basic necessities like food, shelter and fodder, apart from providing us many other advantages that are either direct or indirect. They provide us fruits of different shapes, colours and sizes that are nutritive and do not need any recommendation for their use by the mankind. Apart from man, they are food providers for the birds and animals. Houses and many other buildings are constructed with the help of wood from the trees. In the easiest way, a hut can be made from the bamboo by joining the strips and covering it with the grass. This provides shelter and this does not need any air conditioner or any warming device. In fact, our whole life style is centred on the trees; the advantages of trees have been discussed in this book in detail.

We take almost for guarantee that trees are our own private property and wealth that will never fall short but now the time has come to realize that we have to have more number of trees to cover the earth surface to protect it from degradation. Ways and means have been suggested in this book to get success with the plantation of trees in the places where we feel that trees may not grow.

Thus, it has become our duty to let the nature be in its own way and we should live in harmony with nature and should not unnecessarily exploit the natural wealth, the trees in a way that is injurious both for the mankind and the nature.

In the end I am thankful to my friends and Shri Sarvajit, for providing assistance in the shape of line drawings and help in completing the manuscript so that people are aware of their duties towards the nature.

Shimla DR. V.K. SHARMA

1

CHAPTER

WHY TREES?

Trees are one of the most vital and important resources that nature has bestowed upon the living beings, particularly, the human beings. Trees are woody perennial plants having a single trunk, at least 50 cm above the ground level and then having branches spread all over and the height may be from 3 m to 60 m or so. Trees may be tall like that of pines and junipers while they may be spreading like that of banyan, mango, etc. A tree may be a shrub or a dwarf tree when its height is about 4-5 m. This may be called a bush when the growth is irregular.

Trees occur both in the wild as well as the domesticated form in different corners of the world. They are seen everywhere except the cold deserts and hot deserts where no vegetation is possible due to very harsh soil and climatic conditions.

Perhaps, the trees were meant purely for the purpose of covering the soil and the vegetation beneath them to protect the soil and to help the development and growth of the flora and fauna under the canopy. But man has exploited the use of various kinds of trees for many purposes and they may be :

I. Cover to flora

Under the canopy of a tree, different types of flora have been observed to grow which may include bushes, shrubs, creepers, twining and other vines. Many of these are annual plants, which cover the soil and on their rotting provide organic matter to the trees. Banyan, Pipal, Acacia, Junipers, Conifers, etc., are common trees that provide shelter. Vegetation under these trees remain for years together, their parts fall on the ground, where they decay and enrich the soil and in this way the flora is a supplement which is in symbiotic relation.

2. Shelter to birds and animals

Almost all the birds make their nests on the trees to save their young ones from the attack of animals and other enemies. Hiding place and living place for many of the animals are provided by the trees. Even wild animals take the advantage of the shade of the tree and eat the fruits and buds of the trees.

3. Shelter to human beings

Most of the trees which are shady like Pipal, Mango, Margosa, etc., provide shade to the passerby and a place for resting to many of the villagers and workers. They also protect them from rain, sun and snow in harsh weather. In some cases, trees provide place for hibernation. Normal, tribal and other people have their dwelling under the trees, particularly during summer and rainy season.

4. Beautification of the surroundings

Many tree species are used for landscaping as they have different shapes and habits of growth which may fit in the surroundings. Sometimes, the trees are used as a fence or as a blind to protect the land or to cover up the buildings. With their beautiful leaves, colourful flowers and attractive fruits, they beautify the surroundings. Thuja, Gulmohar, Junipers, Bottle Brush tree, Araucaria, Weeping Willow tree, *Cryptomeria japonica*, etc., are some of the beautiful landscape trees.

5. Utilization of land

Land is a valuable resource which needs to be protected. By planting trees over the land, it is protected from various natural calamities. Rain water which enters into the soil maintains soil moisture in the soil and down below. Same is the case of snow. If these are not conserved, can cause loss to soil surface. In return if utilized properly, it can yield number of benefits. It is the proper utilization of land, which can make it sustainable and higher yield is possible with judicious use of land.

6. Conservation of soil

Soil is exposed to various natural conditions like rain, snow, winds, etc. When in excess, the soil may be washed away or swept away. By growing trees over the soil surface, it protects the soil surface and the roots of the tree bind soil particles together and hence the soil is conserved. No soil loss is possible. Almost all trees are deep rooted and have the spread of roots both horizontally and vertically in the soil.

7. Conservation of soil moisture

Moisture or water is the life-line of all living beings. It provides turgidity to plant, maintains temperature, helps in photosynthesis, respiration, etc. It is essential in many ways. No one may be able to live for more than 24 hours without moisture. In soil, it plays double role. Moisture is essential for the flora and fauna of the soil. It improves the soil conditions, by keeping the soil particles together and helps in decay of organic matter.

8. Improvement in soil conditions

Soil is not merely a mass of minerals, i.e. non-living things but has flora and fauna along with it. This flora and fauna when kept in good conditions help to maintain, rather enrich the soil fertility and maintain the water table in the sub-soil. This maintains the physical, chemical and biological status of the soil.

9. Maintenance of pleasant climate

It is a common phenomenon when there are more trees, the local climate is slightly better than the surroundings but when it is a forested (densely planted) area, climate almost remains pleasant due to shade and conservation of moisture by the trees. Eucalyptus and poplar trees are raised for fast growth to have pleasant climate.

10. Regulation of water cycle

Water is continuously used by trees for manufacture of food and to be in a position to stand erect. Generally, photosynthesis (process of food manufacture) and transpiration (loss or evaporation of water from plant) take place during the day, water is absorbed from the soil and is lost to the atmosphere through transpiration which goes for cloud formation and the same is returned in the form of rain and snow. Thus, there is a regulation of water-cycle for the benefit of living beings.

11. Supply of raw products

Many small scale and large scale industries are dependent upon trees. They obtain raw materials from trees. Plywood, hardboard, pre-fabricated wooden doors, etc., are made out of the wood of the trees. Resins, gums, pulp, oil seeds, bark, roots, etc., are used for manufacture of many items of use in commerce.

12. Provide food and other essential products for living beings

Buds, leaves, fruits, seeds, bark, roots, etc., of the trees are used as food in many ways. They are eaten by mankind, birds, animals and insects. Buds of *Bauhinia variegata* are used as vegetable and pickling : leaves of many trees are used as fodder; fruits like mango, apple, pear, plum, apricot, peach, etc., are used by human beings and animals in a number of ways. Seeds of Jack-fruit, almond, apricot, mango, etc., are used as food after roasting. Bark has medicinal use and for tanning while animals eat roots as food. Apart from this, many essential fatty oils are also extracted from various trees. Oil from olive, almond, apricot, etc., is used in cooking and other food preparations. These are also used in toilette, pharmaceutical and cosmetic industries.

13. Enriching the soil by their bio-mass

Trees are always growing and shedding their old or dried parts. In case of evergreen trees, the process is bit slow but in case of deciduous trees, the process is fast. In case of deciduous trees, there is leaf-fall in the autumn season, where all the leaves are shed in that season and new growth appears during spring. Trees also shed their twigs, buds, fruits, seeds, etc., off and on in a normal way. These fall on the ground, being organic in nature, on decay they enrich the soil in organic manner. They return to the soil whatever they have obtained from soil apart from adding food material synthesized by them. Thus, the soil becomes rich in fertility.

14. Provide aesthetic and psychological satisfaction

People go to the forests, groves, orchards and like places to have their aesthetic and psychological hunger satisfied. Beautiful and colourful parts of the trees in different seasons provide unaccounted satisfaction and boundless psychological satisfaction to the on-lookers, poets, thinkers, etc. Artists and painters do get lot of new ideas and source material for their creations based on the trees and their surroundings. Jacaranda, *Delonix regia*, mango, ash, spruce, fir, cedar, *Cyptomeria japonica*, cupruss, magnolia, etc., are highly ornamental and good avenue trees.

15. Protect environmental pollution

Trees as a rule consume or utilize the waste products, in gaseous form to convert them into useful material. They utilize carbon dioxide and water to synthesize carbohydrates, fats, proteins, etc. Apart from this, trees keep the environment clean. They purify the environment by utilizing various harmful gases. Trees maintain the equilibrium between the useful and harmful gases in nature. It has been reported that the air passing through some trees may relieve the patient of some diseases and provide him freshness.

16. Trees are sacred

Since trees are useful in many ways. They are worshipped by many communities. Tree worship is a tradition with us since times immemorial. Some trees are mostly planted near religious places like temples and other common places. Such trees are banyan, pipal, mango, neem, bael, mulberry, etc.

17. Source of energy

Trees and plants are the living laboratories of nature for the manufacture of carbohydrates and other foods for us. They use the solar energy to convert it into real energy needed by us. This is possible due to the ability of plants to have photosynthesis. Whole of the energy of world is due to plants. No life may be possible without energy received through this source.

18. Generation of employment

Trees provide employment/work to many categories of people. This may be direct or indirect. There are number of industries which are directly dependent upon the forest/trees while others are indirectly dependent. Starting from the basic industry, i.e. the maintenance of trees, in which many departments and people are engaged, is one of the avocations that provide work. For removal of trees, its logging, transportation, disposal of timber, etc., large number of people are associated. Honey, silk, lac, gums, resins, etc., are obtained from the trees. There are number of people involved in this. Apart form this, there are persons employed in raising of nursery plants, transport and conversion of wood into pulp, and in pharmaceutical and cosmetic industries based on forest products.

19. Source of income

Directly trees provide fruits and seeds for human consumption and animal use. These are sold in the market, which brings income to the owner. On their removal, the wood is used in a number of ways, e.g. manufacture of furniture, packing cases, chests, doors, wheel-carts, parts of agricultural implements, plywood, hard-board, pre-fabricated wood, etc. These do bring lot of money as the last value of trees. Raw materials for production of industrial, medicinal, pharmaceutical, domestic preparations and many other products are obtained from the trees. Trees provide place for cultivation of some herbs and medicinal plants. In every respect, trees are valuable for the living beings.

Thus, there are innumerable benefits of trees which can be derived from them but it is the judicious use which can sustain them and bring economic prosperity to us.

USES OF TREES BASED ON THEIR PARTS

Generally trees have various parts that are available for use by the animal kingdom for their use in many ways. These parts are roots, trunks, bark, leaves, flowers, fruits and seeds. Every part of the tree is useful in one or the other way. Important uses of each part are discussed here in general.

Roots

Roots of the trees penetrate deep into the soil and sub-soil, and keep the soil particles binding, thus protecting the soil erosion. These roots provide anchorage to the tree to stand in all types of weather vagaries. Roots go deep or to the sides in search of water that indirectly provides anchorage to the trees. Roots of many of the trees are used in various medicinal and other uses. On the death of a tree, these roots work as capillaries for water to flow downward. Still ahead, these roots on their decay provide organic matter to the soil, thus enriching or at least maintaining the soil fertility.

Canopy

The canopy of the tree i.e., foliage plus the branches, reduce the impact of raindrops on the soil. The raindrops directly fall on the foliage and later after wetting them; these come down to the soil after being reduced in their impact, and then go deep into the soil. When raindrops fall directly on the soil particle, some of the fine particles are disturbed and the soil or hardpan below is exposed and that become nude to face the weathering but the fine soil particles are displaced thus causing the soil to become infertile.

The speed of rain is directly correlated to the soil erosion, higher the speed, more is the soil erosion. This process brings the hard pan to the top or exposed. When there is collection of rainwater i.e., the quantity is more than the capacity of the soil to retain it and that starts flowing as gravitational water which is over and above the hygroscopic water and the capillary water. This flow again leads to soil erosion. Here the slope and speed of rain water are directly related to the amount of soil erosion.

Leaves

Trees have leaves of various shapes, colours and sizes that attract the onlookers and provide beauty to the landscape. They are used in a number of ways. They are used as fodder to cattle and other animals, and are also used as dyeing material. Leaves of many specie of trees are used in preparation of different medicines and other pharmaceutical preparations. They provide shelter and shade to the flora and fauna beneath. On their decay, they add organic matter to the soil. When they drop from the trees, particularly, in deciduous trees, they work as cushion for the raindrops. These are collected and composted or used for making Farm Yard Manure.

Bark

Though bark is meant for protection for the inner tissues of the stem of a tree but in some cases, this is split to make place for the new bark to replace the older bark. In some specie, bark exfoliates. In case of walnut, Margosa, Mahua, etc., the bark has medicinal value. Bark is also used as dyeing and tanning material. The dead wood is used for burning and providing cushion to the floor.

Twigs

These are tender shoots and used as toothbrushes by many of the people living in the villages and small towns. Twigs of Acacia spp., are mostly used for this purpose. Some also use the twigs of Margosa tree for this purpose. Spiny shoots are used for fencing. Shoots after lopping are used as fuel wood.

Buds and Flowers

Buds either give rise to flowers and or leaves. Leaves are used in many ways that have been described in the above paragraph. Flowers are of various shapes and colours so look beautiful and attractive to the human beings and insects, particularly the honeybees and other friendly insects. Flowers on successful pollination and fertilization yield fruits that are used for various purposes. Flowers are meant for fruit formation to provide seeds for multiplication of trees. Buds of *Bauhinia variegata* are used as vegetable. They are also fed to cattle. Flowers of Rhododendron are used for making squash and jam. Flowers may be used for decoration, etc.

Fruits

Again fruits are of various shapes, colours, tastes and aroma that may be good for human consumption. Fruit trees like apple, mango, olive, pomegranate, citrus spp., Terminalia spp., etc. are used for human consumption. Many preparations are made from the fruits that are highly nutritive and refreshing. Some may be dried for use as dry fruits like, grape, almonds, walnut, apricot, etc. Mango powder, Anardana (dried seeds with arils of pomegranate), etc. are also products of trees. Many of the tree specie yield fruits used as medicines.

Seeds

These are mostly used for propagation purposes. Generally, all the trees are multiplied through their seeds that are borne on them. Mature and healthy seeds produce healthy and vigorous plants. Seeds of some specie are used as dry fruits and some for medicines.

Trunk and Branches

Both these provide material for construction. Poles, planks, boards, sleepers, boats, parts of ships, furniture etc., are made from the wood of the trees. Plywood, hardboard, pre-fabricated boards, etc. are also prepared from the leftover wood. Material for packing cases and cabinets are also collected from these portions. On death of the tree, these are used for firewood and logs.

Thus, every part of the tree is valuable for us. Tree as a single unit provides aesthetic satisfaction to many people. They provide food, shelter and place for birds to make their nests. Trees enhance the economic value of the land and the surrounding areas. They enrich the soil fertility and improve texture and structure of the soil. Other advantages of the trees have been described earlier in this chapter.

2

CHAPTER

KINDS OF TREES

Trees are found growing in their natural habitat i.e., natural forests or man-made forests or plantations which have different kinds of trees, they vary in their shape, size, colour of foliage, flowers and fruits. They also differ in their habit of growth and many other characters; thus, we have different classes of trees in this country. Many of them have adjusted themselves to different agroclimatic conditions and as such they are found growing in different regions and locations.

Some of the trees growing in their wild conditions have been domesticated for use in many forms, like fuel, fodder, timber, food, fibre, medicinal, etc. Those trees that have been domesticated and planted by man in his vicinity have become part of the Social forestry, Agro-forestry, etc., these have been adopted for commercial purposes since they play very important role in socio-economic development of the inhabitants

Generally, trees may be classified in a number of ways like the seasonal classification, economic classification, botanical classification, etc.

SEASONAL CLASSIFICATION

They may be deciduous or evergreen according to their nature of shedding leaves.

Deciduous Trees

These trees shed their leaves once a year, mostly in the late autumn or early winter so that they can remain leafless and have their dormancy or rest period. Their leaves emerge during early spring. Sometimes, leaves and flowers appear at the same time but in general, leaves appear first and are followed by flowers. Their growing season is mostly limited to spring and summer while winter is for rest.

Common deciduous trees are:

Apple, pear, peach, plum, apricot, walnut, pecan-nut, persimmon, almond, Horse Chest Nut, Mulberry, Eucalyptus, Poplar, etc.

Evergreen Trees

Trees of this class do not shed their leaves in a particular season and they retain their leaves throughout the year and they are always with leaves. They shed their older leaves off and on to give place for the younger leaves and as such, they do not become leafless. They do not have to go for the dormancy.

Common evergreen trees are:

Different kinds of *Citrus* spp., *mango, Silver Oak, Rubber plant, Jackfruit, palms, casuarina, magnolia, Junipers, Deodar, Cassia, etc.*

ECONOMIC CLASSIFICATION

This classification is based on the utility of the tree for human or other purposes that may include from beautification of the surroundings to availability of fruits and seeds. Some of the economic uses are—food for human consumption, birds, animals, fuel, fodder, timber, shelter, landscaping, honey, medicines, oils and other extracts and seeds for multiplication of plants.

Landscape Trees

These trees are used for improving the landscape of a particular place or site. A tree can be planted in the centre of a lawn or on the side of path or road. They may even be planted to cover a building or any shabby site. They are mostly matched to the background of the site. Such trees are mostly evergreen as the deciduous trees shed their leaves that provide a bad look at that time.

Important landscape trees are:

Delonix regia, Melia azedarach, Madhuca indica, Acacia spp., *Cassia fistula, Mangifera indica, Ficus religiosa, Terminalia arjuna, Jacaranda acutifolia, Saraca indica, Magnolia* spp., *etc.*

Avenue Trees

Trees planted along the paths are known as the Avenue trees. In foreign countries, the names of avenues are based on the type of trees grown there. Apart from matching with the background, these trees provide beauty and grace to the surrounding. Here usually trees of a single species are planted in dense plantation or in a block in a planned way.

Some avenue trees are:

Cedrus deodara, Grevillea robusta, Jacaranda acutifolia, Magnolia, Mangifera indica, Pinus spp., *etc.*

Fruit Trees

Trees of this class may be in isolation or in groups, if planted in a systematic manner add beauty to the place apart from providing fruits for human consumption. There are large number of fruit trees that are being cultivated on commercial scale while other fruit trees are growing wild in scattered locations on marginal lands and wastelands. The fruits from these trees provide food and nutrition to the consumers.

Major fruit trees are:

Papaya, mango, apple, peach, plum, guava, pear, apricot, lemon, lime, mandarin, Sweet Orange, cherry, sapota, pomegranate, persimmon, litchi, loquat, etc.

Timber Trees

Timber is an important item for our social and economic development. It is required in different ways for household, office, commercial and industrial use. It is needed for the sustainable living of the human beings.

Trees providing timber are:

Mangifera indica, Eucalyptus spp., *Juglans regia, Acacia* spp., *Ziyzyphus* spp., *Poplar spp.,* etc.

Fuel Trees

Ruralites living near the forests are dependent on fuel from forests. They have adjusted their daily routine in such a way that they are unable to do without this. Fuel is needed for cooking of food in all seasons and fuel for warming up in the winter. No other alternative for fuel is available in remote areas. They also sell this to other people who are not able to collect them. Thus, it is a necessary evil for the time being.

Trees providing fuel are:

Prosopis juliflora, Albizia lebbek, Tamarindus indica, Robinia pseudoacaia, etc.

Fodder Trees

Fodder is an essential item for the feeding of animals, particularly those that are stall-fed. In hills, land is limited and so is the availability of grass, growers are not able to get the fodder for their cattle and other animals because of the limitations of the season and the soil. Nature has provided solution to this, as there are some species that yield fodder that is both nutritive and good for all classes of animals.

Important fodder yielding trees are:

Salix tetrosperma, Robinia pseudoacacia, Celtis australis, Populus ciliata, Bauhinia variegata, Sesbania grandifolia, Zizyphus jujube, Acacia spp., *Ficus* spp., *Prosopis julifera, etc.*

Medicinal Trees

Many trees yield products that are used by tribal and other people for the healing and treatment of various diseases and ailments. Leaves of the trees of *Aegle marmelos, Mangifera indica, Zizyphus mauritiana, Azadirachta indica,* etc., are used for various pharmaceutical purposes. Flowers, seeds, fruits, the physicians against various abnormalities use roots, bark, twigs, etc. for human and animals.

Other trees of this category are: *Terminalia bellirica, Terminalia chebula, Tamarindus indica, Syzygium cumini, Emblica officianlis, Ficus religiosa, Ficus benghalensis, Carica papaya,* Cinchona, Cinnamon tree, Camphor tree, etc.

Honey Trees

Some of the trees bear flowers of many colours that have fragrance to attract the honey-bees. Honeybees collect nectar from the flowers of these trees and manufacture honey for use by their offsprings and the human beings.

Some of the sweet smelling and attractive flowers are—Specie of *Dalbergia, Terminalia, Albizzia, Eucalyptus, Berberis, Morus, Acacia,* etc.

Trees for Oil and Other Extracts

Thess type of trees yield oils meant for industrial, domestic, pharmaceutical, toiletry, cosmetic and other uses. Rubber, resin, katha, and other products are extracted from this type of trees.

Common trees of this class are—Pinus spp., apricot, *Acacia catechu, Madhuca indica, etc.*

Windbreak Trees

These trees help in checking the speed of flow of air current. Hot current of air increases the rate of transpiration of water from the trees and evaporation from the earth or ground. Cold winds cause freezing of cell sap within the plant leading to rupturing of tissues and finally the death of tissues. Planting trees that have the capacity to check the flow of air speed checks both these types of currents. These trees are evergreen, have enough foliage, their growth is fast and they start branching near the earth surface.

Cydonia vulgaris, Citrus spp., *Dalbergia sissoo*, Mulberry, Eucalyptus, Poplar, Jamun, etc. are planted close to the boundary of the site by keeping less distance between the trees. There can be one or two rows of such trees to check the speed of flow of current and to trap the sand particles from swaying.

Apart from these types of trees, there are trees that provide shelter, shade, aesthetic beauty and many other advantages to the human kind and animals.

BOTANICAL CLASSIFICATION

Plant kingdom has been classified on the basis of order, family, genera and species so that they can be identified easily. Trees belonging to one particular family have some characters, which are common in that class but the trees or plants having some specific characteristics have been classed under specific genera and specie. Important families are:

Annonaceae—Annona squamosa, Mangifera indica, Polyalthia longifolia.

Apocynaceae—Carissa carandas.

Bignoniaceae—Jacaranda mimosaefolia, Millingtonia hortensis.

Bombaceae—Bombax malabaricum.

Boraginaceae—Cordia myxa.

Caricaceae—Carica papaya.

Casuarianaceae—Casuarina equisetifolia.

Combretaceae—Terminalia spp.

Cupressaceae—Cupressus spp.

Ebernaceae—Diospyros spp.

Ericaceae—Rhododendron spp.

Euphorbiaceae—Phyllanthus emblica, Sapium detergens, Sapium sebiferum, Manihot esculanta.

Fagaceae—Quercus spp.

Juglandaceae—Juglan regia, Carya illinoiensis.

Lauraceae—Cinnamonum camphora, Cinnamomum tamala, Persea ameriacana.

Lythraceae—Lagerstroemia flos-reginae.

Meliaceae—Melia azedarach, Melia superba, Azadirachta indica.

Mimosaceae—Prosopis juliflora, Albizzia spp.

Moraceae—Ficus religiosa, Ficus benghalensis, Ficus carica, Morus alba, Morus nigra.

Myrtaceae—Callistemon lanceolatus, Eucalyptus spp., *Eugenia cuspidata, Eugenia jambolana.*

Oleaceae—Olea europea, Olea cuspidata.

Palmae—Arenga pinnata, Phoenix dactylifera, Areca catechu, Cocos nucifera.

Papilionaceae—Sesbania grandiflora.
Pinaceae—Pinus spp., *Fir, Cedar.*
Proteaceae—Grevillea robusta.
Punicaceae—Punica granatum.
Rhamnaceae—Zizyphus spp.
Rosaceae—Prunus persica, Prunus avium, Prunus domestica, Malus domestica, Pyrus pashia, Pyrus communis, Eriobotrya japonica.
Rubiaceae—Anthocephalus cadamba, Coffea arabica, Coffea robusta.
Rutaceae—Citrus spp., *Murraya exotica. Aegle marmelos.*
Salicaceae—Poplar spp.
Sapindaceae—Aesculus indica.
Solanaceae—Nicotiana tabacum.
Taxodiaceae—Cryptomeria japonica.
Verbenaceae—Tectona grandis.

3

CHAPTER

DISTRIBUTION OF TREES

Trees are found throughout the country in various regions according to requirements of their basic need, i.e. climatic conditions. They may be temperate, tropical or sub-tropical depending upon the region in which they grow.

Temperate region has cool climatic and is mountainous having high hills. During winter the temperature goes below the freezing point of water i.e., –4°C. These areas are specifically under the Himalayas and other high mountain ranges, and experience snow-fall during winter. As such under harsh winter, only hardy plants can survive.

Tropical region is around the tropics and quite hot during summer, the temperature goes beyond 50°C, here hot deserts are common which may cause the temperature during the night to fall much below average temperature and is usually around 10°C.

Sub-tropical region has the areas which fall in between the temperate and tropical regions, i.e. there are rains during winter and in rainy season, and the average temperature hovers between 15°-40°C. In such areas, there are foothills and valleys.

CLIMATIC FOREST TYPES

Champion and Seth (1967) have differentiated the following 16 climatic forest types in the country.

1. Tropical Wet Evergreen Forest

Lofty, very dense, multi-layered forest with mesophytic evergreens, 45 m or more high with a large number of specie, numerous epiphytes, few climbers. Found along the western face of the Western Ghats and in a strip running South-West Upper Assam through Cachar, and in Andamans.

(i) Kerala, 1000 m.

Important spp. Mesua, White Cedar, Calophyllum, Toon, Dhup, Palaquium, Hopea, Jamun, Canes, etc.

(ii) Cachar, Assam

Important spp. Gurjan, Chaplash, Jamun, Mesua, Agar, Muli, Bamboo, etc.

2. Tropical Semi-Evergreen Forest

A closed high forest with large dominants, sometimes deciduous, with tendency to gregariousness, many specie, buttressed trunks frequent, bark thicker and rougher and canopy less dense than in previous type, climbers heavy, bamboos less prevalent, epiphytes abundant. Occurs in the Western Coast, Assam, lower slopes of the Eastern Himalayas, Orissa and in Andamans.

(i) Kerala

Important spp. Aini, Semul, Gutel, Mundani, Hopea, Benteak, Kadamba, Irul, Laurel, Rosewood, Mesua, Haldu, Kanju, Bijasal, Kusum, Thorny Bamboo, etc.

(ii) Kalimpong, W. Bengal

Important spp. Bonsum, White Cedar, Indian Chestnut, Litsea, Holloch, Champa, Mango, etc.

3. Tropical Moist Deciduous Forest

Irregular top storey of predominantly deciduous specie, 40 m or more high, heavily buttressed trees, definite second storey of many specie with some evergreens, fairly complete shrubby undergrowth with patches of bamboos, climbers heavy including canes. Occurs throughout Andamans, moister parts of Uttar Pradesh, Madhya Pradesh, Gujarat, Maharashtra, Karnataka and Kerala.

(i) Andamans

Important spp. Padauk, White Chuglam, Badam, Dhup, Chikrasi, Kokko.

(ii) Maharashtra

Important spp. Teak, Laurel, Haldu, Rosewood, Mahua, Bijasal,

Lendi, Semul, Irul, Dhaman, Garari, Amla, Kusum, Common bamboo, etc.

(iii) Uttaranchal

Important spp. Sal, Lendi, Haldu, Pula, Litsea, Jamun, Mahul, etc.

4. Littoral and Swamp Forest

Mainly evergreen specie of varying density and height, always associated with wetness; Littoral forests are found all along the coast and swamp forests in the deltas of bigger rivers.

(i) West Bangal

Important spp. Sundri, Bruguiera, Sonneratia, Agar, Bhendi, Keora, Nipa, etc.

5. Tropical Dry Deciduous Forest

Upper canopy closed though rather uneven, composed of a mixture of a few specie practically all deciduous during the dry season, some for several months, upto 20 m high, some specie tend to predominate over selected areas but most non-gregarious, lower canopy almost entirely deciduous, shrubs present but enough light reaches the forest floor to permit growth of grass; bamboos present unless exterminated by over cutting but not luxuriant, climbers few but some large and woody, epiphytes and ferns inconspicuous. Occurs in an irregular wide strip running NS from the foot of the Himalayas to Cape Comorin except in Rajasthan, Western Ghats and Bengal.

(i) Madhya Pradesh

Important spp. Teak, Axlewood, Tendu, Bijasal, Rosewood, Amaltas, Palas, Haldu, Kasi, Bael, Lendi, Common bamboo, etc.

(ii) Andhra Pradesh

Important spp. Red Sanders, Axlewood, Anjan, Harra, Laurel, Stainwood, Papra, Achar, etc.

(iii) Uttaranchal

Important spp. Sal, Laurel, Axlewood, Bhilama, Achar, Khair, Ghont, Bael, etc.

6. Tropical Thorn Forest

Open, low, pronouncedly xerophytic forest, thorny leguminous specie predominate, trees with short boles and low branches, an ill-defined lower storey of smaller trees and shrubs, spiny and with xerophytic characteristics, climbers few. This type grows in a large strip in South Punjab, Rajasthan, Upper Gangetic Plains, the Deccan Plateau and the lower peninsular India.

(i) Maharashtra

Important spp. Khair, Reunjha, Axlewood, Neem, Sandalwood, Nirmali, Dhaman, etc.

(ii) Rajasthan

Important spp. Acacia senegal, Reunjha, Khejra, Neem, Palas, Ak, etc.

7. Tropical Dry Evergreen Forest

A low forest, upto 12 m high with complete canopy, mostly of coriaceous leaved evergreen trees of short boles, no canopy layer differentiation, bamboos rare or absent, grass not conspicuous. Restricted to a small area of Karnataka Coast which receives some summer rain also.

Important spp. Khirni, Jamun, Kokko, Ritha, Tamarind, Neem, Machkund, Toddy Palm, Gamari, Canes, etc.

8. Sub-Tropical Broad-Leaved Hill Forest

Luxuriant forest evergreen specie predominating limited to the lower slopes of the Himalayas in Bengal and Assam and other hill ranges such as Khasi, Nilgiri and Mahableshwar.

Important spp. Jamun, Machilus, Meliosma, Elaeocarpus, Celtis, *australis*, etc.

9. Sub-Tropical Pine Forest

Practically pure association of Chir Pine, considerably influenced by periodical fires, no underwood, few shrub. Found throughout the whole length of North Western Himalayas between 1000-1800 m. Absent in Kashmir due to weakened South-West monsoon. In Khasi, Manipur and Naga Hills, Khasya pine occurs at similar altitudes.

(i) Uttaranchal

Important spp. Chir, Jamun, Oak, Rhododendron, etc.

10. Sub-Tropical Dry Evergreen Forest

Low, practically scrub forest, small evergreen stunted trees and shrubs including thorny species, herbs and grasses appear in monsoon, Met with in the Bhabar, the Shiwaliks and the Western Himalayas upto about 1000 m.

Important spp. Olive, *Acacia modesta*, Pistacia, etc.

11. Montane Wet Temperate Forest

A closed evergreen forest. Trees mostly short-boled and branchy, attaining large girth, height rarely 6 m, crowns dense and rounded leaves coriaceous, red when young, branches clothed with mosses, ferns and other epiphytes. Woody climbers common. Found in the higher hills of Tamil Nadu and Kerala from 150 m upwards and in Eastern Himalayas on the higher hills of Bengal, Assam and North Eastern States from 1800 to 3000 m.

Important spp. Machilus, Cinnamon, Litsea, Magnolia, Chilauni, Indian Chestnut, Birch, Plum.

12. Himalayan Moist Temperate Forest

Coniferous forest, mostly pure, 30 to 50 m high with varying, underwood mostly evergreen, mosses and ferns grow freely on trees. Extends along the entire length of the Himalayas between the pine and the sub-alpine forests in Kashmir, Himachal Pradesh, Punjab, Uttaranchal, Darjeeling and Sikkim between 1,500 and 3,300 m.

(i) Chakrata, Uttaranchal

Important spp. Oak, Fir, Spruce, Deodar, Celtis, *australis* Chestnut, Maple, etc.

(ii) Sutlej Valley, Himachal Pradesh

Important spp. Spruce, Deodar, Fir, Kail, Oak, Yew, Maple, Birch, etc.

13. Himalayan Dry Temperate Forest

Predominantly coniferous forest with xerophytic shrubs, hardly any epiphytes and climbers. Found in the inner ranges of the Himalayas where South-Western monsoon is very feeble, precipitation below 100 mm, mostly snow; on Ladakh, Lahaul, Chamba, Kinnaur, Garhwal and Sikkim.

U. Bushahar, Himachal Pradesh

Important spp. Chilgoza, Deodar, Oak, Maple, Ash, Celtis, *australis* Parrotia, Olive, etc.

14. Sub-Alpine Forest

Dense growth of small crooked trees or large shrubs with coniferous overwood, mostly fir and birch. Conifers 30 m high, broad-leaved trees 10 m high. Occurs at the upper limit of tree forest in the Himalayas adjoining alpine scrub and grasslands.

Himachal Pradesh

Important spp. Fir, Pine, Spruce, Rhododendron, Plum, Yew, etc.

15. Moist Alpine Scrub

Low evergreen dense growth of Rhododendron and Birch. Mosses and ferns on the ground with alpine shrubs and flowering herbs. Occurs along the entire length of Himalayas above 3000 m.

Kuman, Uttaranchal 3,800 m

Important spp. Birch, Rhododendron, Berberis, Honeysuckle, etc.

16. Dry Alpine Scrub

The uppermost limit of scrub xerophytic, dwarf shrubs, over about 3,500 meters.

High Himalayas .over 4,000 m

Important spp. Juniper, Honeysuckle, Artemesia, Potentilla, etc.

PHYSICAL FEATURES

There are three well-defined regions in the country that mark the type of the trees and the specie, which grow under different agroclimatic conditions. Following are the three regions:

(i) *Himalayan Zone*: This comprises of the main forested area that is natural and only part of that has been disturbed by mankind and natural calamities.

(ii) *Indo-Gangetic Plain*: This is a strip of about 2400 km long and 240 to 320 km broad forming the basins of the rivers like Indus, Ganga and Brahmaputra. It is highly fertile and therefore very densely populated.

(iii) *Deccan Peninsula* : This is a plateau with a mass of mountain and hill ranges, 450-1200 m high. The most prominent being the Aravalli, the Vindhya, the Satpura, the Maikal, and the Ajanta. Eastern Ghat have an average elevation of 600 m while the Western Ghats have an average elevation of 900-1200 m. Both of them join the South forming the high Nilgiri Plateau. Between the Arabian Sea and the Western Ghats, there is a narrow coastal strip while the area between the Eastern Ghats and the Bay of Bengal is considerably broad.

Following is a list of the common trees growing in various parts:

List of Useful Trees

Botanical Name	*English Name*	*Local Name*
Abies pindrow	Fir	Tosh
Acacia arabica		Kikar, Babool
Acacia catechu	Cutch tree	Khair
Acacia modesta		Phalahi
Acer caesium	Maple	Trekhon
Adina cordifolia		Haldu
Aegle marmelos		Bael, Bilva
Aesculus indica	Horse Chest Nut	Pangar, Khanor
Ailanthus excelsa		Arru, Maharukh
Albizia chinensis		Siran
Albizia lebbek	East Indian Walnut	Safed Siris
Alnus nepalensis	Alder	Kunish
Anthocephalus cadamba		Kadamba
Artocarpus heterophyllus	Jackfruit tree	Kathal
Artocarpus lakoocha		Dheu
Azadirachta indica	Margosa	Neem
Bauhinia purpurea		Khairwal
Bauhinia vareigata	Orchid Tree	Kachnar
Betula alnoides		Kath
Bombax ceiba	Silk Cotton Tree	Semal
Butea monosperma	Flame of the Forest	Dhak, Palash
Callistemon lanceolatus	Bottle Brush tree	
Carica papaya	Papaya	Papita
Carpinus viminea		Lolti
Carya illinoiensis	Pecan-nut	Pecan
Cassia fistula	Indian Labrnum	Amaltas
Castanea sativa	Spanish Chestnut	
Casuarina equisetifolia	Whistling Pine	Casuarina
Cedrela toona	Red Cedar	Tun, Toon

Cedrus deodara	Himalayan Cedar	Deodar
Celtis australis	European Hackberry	Khirak
Cinnamomum camphora	Camphor tree	Kapur
Cinnamomum tamala	Indian Cassia	Tej Patra
Citrus aurantifolia	Lime	Meetha
Citrus limon	Lemon	Neemboo
Citrus pseudo-limon	Hill lemon	Galgal
Citrus reticulata	Mandarin	
Citrus sinensis	Sweet Orange	
Cryptomeria japonica	Japanese Cedar	Japani Saru
Cydonia vulgaris	Quince	
Dalbegia sissoo		Shisham, Tahli
Delonix regia		Gulmohar
Diospyros kaki	Persimmon	Japani Phal
Diospyros lotus		Amlok
Embilca officinalis	India Gooseberry	Amla, Aonla
Erythrina suberosa	Coral Tree	Pangra
Ficus benghalensis	Banyan tree	Bargad, Borh
Ficus glomerata		Gular
Ficus religiosa	Pipal	Pipal
Ficus roxburghii		Trimala
Fraxinus floribunda	Ash tree	
Grevillea robusta	Silver Oak	
Grewia optiva		Buel
Jacaranda mimosaefolia	Jacaranda	Jacaranda
Juglans regia	Walnut	Akhrot
Juniperus macropoda	Pencil Cedar	
Lagerstroemia parviflora		Dhaura
Lannea coromandelica		Jhingan
Leucaena leucocephala	Leucaena	Sababul
Litchi chinensis	Litchi	Litchi
Mangnolia grandiflora	Magnolia	Bara Champa
Malus domestica	Apple	Seb
Mangifera indica	Mango	Aam, Amb
Melia azedarach	Bead tree	Bakain, Drake
Morus alba	Mulberry	Shehtoot
Morus nigra	Mulberry	Shehtoot
Olea cuspidata	Wild Olive	Kahu
Olea eurpaea	Olive	Zaitun
Ougeinia oojeinensis		Sandan
Persea americana	Avocado Pear	Makhani Phal
Picea smithiana	Western Himalayan Spruce	Rai
Pinus gerardiana		Chilgoza
Pinus roxbughii	Long Leaved Pine	Chir
Platanus orientalis	Chinar	Chinar

Plumeria acutifolia	Pagoda Tree	
Populus spp.	Poplar	Poplar
Prunus amygdalus	Almond	Badam
Prunus armeniaca	Apricot	Khurmani
Prunus avium	Sweet Cherry	Cherry, Glas
Prunus cerasus	Flowering Cherry	
Prunus domestica	European Plum	Alucha
Prunus persica	Peach	Aaroo
Prunus puddum		Paja, Painyan
Prunus saliciana	Japanese Plum	Alubhukhara
Psidium guajava	Guava	Amrood
Punica granatum	Pomegranate	Anar
Pyrus communis	Pear	Nashpati, Nakh
Pyrus pashia		Kainth
Quercus dilata	Oak	Tilonj, Mohru
Quercus glauca	Oak	Phaniyar
Quercus incana	Ban Oak	Banj, Ban
Quercus lanata	Oak	Rianj
Quercus semiecarpiflora	Oak	Kharsu
Rhododendron arboreum	Rhododendron	Bras
Robinia pseudo-acacia	Black Locust Tree	Robinia
Salix babylonica	Willow	Majnu
Sorbus foliolsa	Ash	
Syzygium cuminii	Black Plum, Indian Cherry	Jamun
Taxus baccata	Himalayan Yew	
Tectona grandis	Teak	Sagwan
Terminalia bellirica	Belliric Myrobalan	Bahera
Terminalia chebula	Chebulic Myrobalan	Harar
Terminalia tomentosa	Laurel	Sain, Hasan
Tsuga dumosa	Himalayan Hemlock	Tunsen
Ulmus wallichiana	Elm	Bren, Brera
Zizyphus mauritiana		Ber

Apart from the trees mentioned above, there are number of other species found growing in this part of the country, some of them have been exploited for commercial use while others are growing as wild either in isolation or in clusters. However, there are plantations of trees in many parts.

These trees are not only found growing in forests and adjoining areas but they have been planted at the following sites:

Places and areas of tourists' attraction.

Near religious places like temples, shrines, churches and cremation grounds.

Roadside plantations.

Sides of lakes, water reservoirs and other water bodies including the banks of rivers and streams.

On mined areas for their development.

Places of archeological importance.

Industrial estates.

Educational institutes.

On wasteland and marginal lands, which are not in use for agricultural purposes.

Pastures and grasslands.

Commercial plantations of Eucalyptus and Poplar.

Municipal parks, etc.

4

CHAPTER

MANAGEMENT OF TREES

From the cultural, nutritional and management point of view, different types of trees can be divided into four broad categories. These are, Ornamental trees, Fruit trees, Forest trees and Miscellaneous trees. All trees are vital for humanity and for well-being of all the living beings.

(a) Ornamental Trees

Trees that are raised for beautification or landscaping purposes are known as Ornamental trees. Such trees are planted primarily for making a place attractive. Their leaves, floral parts, i.e., inflorescence, buds, flowers, and other parts are usually colourful, good smelling and decorative to suit the background in which they grow. They are also planted along the roads, paths, canal banks, on landfills and in isolation in parks and gardens. These trees provide shade and shelter to others. Some creepers and soil covering plants do grow under them.

Common landscape trees are—*Delonix regia*, Magnolia, *Cassia fistula*, *Butea monosperma*, Bottle brush, *Cryptomeria japonica*, Horse Chestnut, Flowering Cherry, Aruacaria, Rhododendron, Palms, Cycads, Christmas tree.

(b) Fruit Trees

These trees are mostly raised for their fruits which may be picked at different stages of their development i.e., maturity, depending upon their use in commerce. Fruit trees are generally planted in orchards where they are raised as commercial fruits but few trees can be raised here and there in the farmers' field or in kitchen gardens as a specimen tree. Every fruit tree can not be recommended for kitchen garden as some of them require cross-pollination. This is particularly true for apple, papaya, Kiwi fruit, etc. Guava, mango, litchi, pear, plum, peach, apricot, pomegranate, coconut, citrus, date-palm, chestnut, sapota, walnut, etc., can be grown in orchards as well as in isolation.

These trees provide fruits of various colours, attractive shapes, pleasant flavours, agreeable tastes and of different degree of sweetness and these fruits are nutritive for all. They provide almost all the nutritive elements, vitamins, hormones and enzymes in the most palatable manner. Some of the trees are also of medicinal value like *Emblica offcinalis, Terminalia bellirica, Terminalia chebula, Tamarindus indica, Juglans regia, Aegle marmelos,* date-palm, etc. Wood of these trees, particularly of walnut, apple and chestnut is used in a number of ways. Essential oils, resins, gums, etc., are also extracted from some fruit trees.

(c) Forest Trees

These trees are mostly grown in well-marked regions where they are raised in large number for the purpose of covering the soil and protecting the environment from further degradation. There is large number of trees found growing in the forest, some of the species have not even been common to mankind. Forest may be natural or man-made.

Trees in such areas are raised for timber, wood, oil, gums, resins, seeds, etc. Common trees of this class are oaks, firs, birches, pines, teak, deodar, sandal wood, acacias, poplars, eucalyptus, cassias, etc. Some of them are used for fuel, fodder and other minor uses for the forest dwellers. They are mostly planted on slopes, denudated lands, degraded lands, waste lands and other areas which are not suitable for cultivation of cereals and other crops. Since tree raising is easy, does not need much care after planting, less prone to attack of insects and diseases, people have adopted their plantations on marginal lands. By law, forests are the protected areas and are mostly owned by government but there are some plantations, which are under private ownership.

(d) Miscellaneous Trees

These trees are of less economic importance than the earlier described categories since these are multi-purpose and are useful for the society or community. In fact, these trees are the back-bone of the rural communities who depend upon them for a number of purposes. They get food, fuel, timber, fodder, wood, etc. Basketry, sericulture, lac-culture, making handles of various hand tools, and many other cottage industries are dependent on the wood and other products of forests.

These trees are part of social forestry, agro-forestry and like systems. Some of the trees of this class are important from the religious point of view. *Ficus benghalensis, Ficus religiosa, Aegle marmelos, Zizyphus mauritiana,* Christmas trees are some that are valued for their utility in religion. Other trees of this category are—Bamboo, Mulberry, Leucaena, *Madhuca indica, Syzygium cumini, Grevillea robusta, Saraca indica, Sapium detergens, Azardirachta indica,* Bahera, Amla, Harar, Clove, Cinchona, Cinnamon, nutmeg, indigo, rubber, etc.

Selecting Site

This is the most important aspect which must be viewed carefully before any programme for planting of trees is to be undertaken. Though any site where a plant can find a place to establish itself may be suitable but it must be considered that the future tree has to be there for a period of over 20 years and should get ample opportunities for its full development. One may have to spend lot of money on the watch and ward and supervision of a lonely or an isolated plantation that may be visited by wild animals, birds and other insects. Too windy and too slopy land may require special attention in overcoming these short-comings. For economic and successful tree raising, site should be preferably with a gentle slope, not water-logged, not visited by wild animals, birds and insects, not far away from the habitation, not having harsh climate, often flooded land, where industrial waste has been dumped, and having other short-comings.

For selecting a site for orchard plantation, one may have to consider many other aspects, particularly, nearness to the road and market, availability of inputs, labour and other resources, etc.

It may be difficult to select an ideal site for planting trees of different categories. One has to compromise to get maximum out of the available site and as such one should go for proper selection of specie and soil on a particular site to make the business economical.

Selection of Specie

One should select the species to be raised according to the agro-climatic conditions of the site. Trees of temperate region may be planted at places where they can get sufficient chill to complete their dormancy. They may not be successful in other areas. Similarly, trees of coastal areas like coconut, cashew nut, etc., do not grow well under cool conditions. There are a number of pine and poplar species that can grow from seacoast to alpine region but one has to select the right type of specie that is recommended for particular area.

The purpose of tree husbandry should also be considered carefully. For timber production, one may have to find its market for sale. Further, new specie may not be successful in a new site. Experiences of the neighbourers or experts may have to be taken into account. Availability of technology for cultural practices and then processing of the produce has also to be viewed seriously. It is better not to be the first and the last in this business.

Preparation of Site

First of all, remove the bushes and other weeds from the soil surface. Deep rooted bushes may be cut near the ground level and later their remains may be dug if required. Use of weedicides may be made if necessary. If the land is having steep slope, small terraces may be made or contour-planting method may be adopted. Topography of the soil should not be disturbed. Upper layer of the earth, i.e. soil is more fertile than the sub-soil. Places for planting of trees may be marked by adopting a suitable plan of layout.

There are four methods of layout like Square system, Rectangular system, Hexagonal system and Contour system in common use. Each method has its advantages and disadvantages. System of layout will depend upon the type of soil, slope of the land and the purpose of plantation. Generally, on steep slope sites as in hills and valleys, Contour system is followed while in plains or other areas on flat lands either the Square or Rectangular system is followed. By adopting systematic planning, one can work out the number of trees required for planting and later the yield or quantity of produce from such trees. Distance between two plants should be sufficient for their proper growth and development.

Place for a tree may be marked by putting a wooden peg of white colour (white washed with lime).

Soil and its Preparation

(a) Ornamental Trees

Since the main aim of raising these trees is to have a good landscape, they need a good soil which should be enough rich in fertility to keep the tree in a good condition for a long time, say for 20-30 years or so depending upon the type of the tree and the purpose of its raising.

Generally, clay loam to sandy loam soil is best suited. After marking the place for planting a tree, we have to dig a pit of 1 m^3. First dig the upper layer of about 30 cm of earth, which is soil and keep it in a heap and then remove the lower layer of 70 cm depth, which is sub-soil, keep this in another heap. Both the heaps are exposed to sun for 2 days during which period, the eggs of the insects and remains of diseases are destroyed or killed by exposure to sun and are picked by birds. These two days should be sunny. Generally, the pits are prepared during summer or autumn as these are rain-free days.

After exposure of soil for 2 days, pits are filled. In case, there is an unwanted material in the dug soil, that may be removed. Big stones, etc., may be removed. They may be substituted by good soil from the nearby place. First fill the pit with the sub-soil which was dug later and kept in a separate heap. Now, mix 10-15 kg of well rotten Farm Yard

Manure to the soil (upper layer) and fill the pit. It is mixed well with the soil. Half rotten Farm Yard Manure should not be added as it leads to the attack of White ants and fungus.

During this preparation, one can examine the type of the soil of the pit. In case it is gravely or of other nature, it can be corrected. One may add sand or clay soil to modify the soil of the pit. Too acidic or too alkaline soil should be avoided. Generally, the soil should have pH within the range of 5 to 6.5. One can also see that there is no hard pan in or around the pit.

In case the soil is poor in fertility, 250 g of Superphosphate and 150 g of Muriate of Potash per pit may be mixed with the soil.

A pit that has been filled as described here, will be having a doam shaped appearance. The top layer is pressed with the back of shovel or feet and should have an outward slope so that the rain water may go off. In the centre of the pit, again the peg is fixed.

Pits prepared during summer will be ready to receive the plants during monsoon and may not need any watering. Similarly, the pits prepared during the autumn season will be ready in winter. The time gap of one and a half month to two months will be sufficient for the manures and fertilizers to decompose and become in the available form for the young plants. Moreover, one has to prepare many pits during the season, so the farmer or owner can utilize the labour efficiently for this purpose.

(b) Fruit Trees

For orchard plantation, pits are to be dug and filled as for ornamental trees. Quantity of manure and fertilizers to be added to the soil will depend upon the type of the tree and the soil. Since these trees are raised for fruit production, they need good fertile soil and ample dose of fertilizers and manures.

20 kg of well rotten Farm Yard Manure, 250 g of Super phosphate and 125 g of Muriate of Potash are mixed with the top layer of pit at the time of preparation of pit. Half dose of nitrogenous fertilizer, generally CAN (Calcium ammonium nitrate) is mixed with the soil, few days (7 to 10) before the transplanting of trees. As a thumb rule, 100 g of CAN per pit may be mixed before transplanting of trees.

(c) Forest Trees

Normally for forest trees, no pits are prepared. In flat areas, the soil is worked by a furrow turning plough and a digger is run in a line where the tree will be. In hills, there is contour plantation, small pits (equal to the size of roots or spread of roots) are dug to place the plants.

As a general practice, pit of 45-60 cm depth may be dug and filled prior to transplanting. This will ensure the quality of soil and will provide better conditions for the spread of roots. Mostly the pits are prepared equal to the spread of roots of plant and plants are put in pits, since the number of trees to be planted is more and these do not need much care as the ornamental or fruit trees.

For commercial plantation of Eucalyptus, Poplar and teak trees, pits of convenient sizes may be prepared earlier. Organic manure like the Farm Yard Manure, Compost, Green manure, etc., may be mixed. To have better growth of these trees, one may use some quantity of CAN as a top dressing.

(d) Miscellaneous Trees

Here, again the pits are rarely prepared since the use of these trees is for domestic purposes and they get some dose of manure after they have been planted. It is worthwhile to have a pit so that the future tree may be vigorous and should yield quality produce. Under social forestry or agro-forestry systems, trees are planted in lines along with the main crop. These are perennial and hence are not cared much. These get the manure and inter-culture from the main crop. It is advantageous to have pits of atleast 60 cm depth. Depending upon the kind of the tree, some quantity, say about 10 kg of well rotten Farm Yard Manure, should be added and mixed well with the soil.

As a precautionary measure, one must add and mix 20-25 g of BHC, Aldrin or some other insecticide to the soil of the pit before transplanting to avoid the attack of insects. Moreover, well rotten Farm Yard Manure or Compost must be added to each pit at the time of its preparation to have good growth of the trees, irrespective of the kind of the tree and the purpose of its plantation. A virgin soil may not need manure but other soils do need. To get a virgin soil, these days it is impossible because we have already over exploited the good soil. Now wastelands, marginal lands, barren, slopy and like lands are available for tree plantation.

RAISING A PLANT

Plant raising is an art. There are three essential things for raising a plant, seed, soil and its environment. In general, seeds are sown which on germination and growth by getting suitable conditions become independent plants. Sometimes, in place of seed, stem or root cuttings are used for preparing new plants. In place of ordinary soil, some substitute may also be used but that is to a limited extent. The environment includes the air, moisture, temperature, light, etc. All these conditions have to be congenial for raising a new plant.

Seed

It is the most important part of the plant meant for multiplication. Seeds are produced in large number and are well protected against climate odds. Well mature seeds are collected from healthy and vigorous trees. These are cleaned and then stored in dry and cool place. Later, they are placed for germination during a particular season.

Plants are also able to propagate themselves by other means like cuttings, may be from stems, roots or leaves but generally stem cuttings are used. There are some other plant parts or modification of parts that can be used for raising new plants.

Seed and other material meant for multiplication should be healthy, disease and insect free. It should be true to its vegetative and reproductive characters and should present the desirable or representative characteristics of the specie or variety. Above all, they should provide vigorous growth.

Selection of seed

Seed for sowing should be selected carefully. It must have the representative characteristics of a particular species in terms of its weight, colour, boldness, shape, size, shine, etc. It should neither be too old nor too raw but it should be well matured.

Seed sowing

Healthy seeds are sown in well-prepared beds, trays or pots having fertile and pulverised soil which has ample moisture.

Depth of seeding is kept according to the size of the seed, usually three times the breadth of the seed. They may be either spread or dibbled. After uniform spreading, they are covered with a layer of soil so that they are not exposed to natural vagaries and are not picked by birds, etc. If possible, do apply light irrigation.

Bigger seeds like that of mango (seed-stone), coconut (nut), apricot, almond, peach, plum, cherry, walnut, pecan-nut, etc., are sown directly. Sometimes these seeds are sown *in situ,* i.e. they are not raised in a bed but sown in the pit.

Seeds that require special treatments before germination are treated properly. Dormant seeds of temperate trees are provided chilly conditions to complete their dormancy, seeds having fuzz are rubbed in dry cow dung or sand to separate them.

It is better to treat the seeds with a suitable fungicide before planting so that they are not attacked by fungus.

Spacing between two seeds has to be appropriate. This will depend on the size of the seed. Small seeds are placed 2 cm apart while bold seeds are placed 5 cm apart. In the seedbed, seeds are sown 3-5 cm apart and later the seedlings are thinned.

Germination of seeds

Soon after planting, the seed absorbs moisture form the soil, swells up, embryo is activated which sends radical and plumule to form roots and stem, respectively to form young sapling or seedling. It may take 7-10 days or so depending upon the specie.

Planting of cuttings

Generally cuttings from one-year-old shoots are taken for planting. These are usually 10-12 cm long having 1 cm diameter with 2-3 buds. Season of their collection and planting depends upon the nature of specie. Deciduous trees are planted in winter while evergreen trees are planted just on the onset of monsoon season. Fresh cuttings are preferred for planting. These are cut with a secateure. Upper end above the bud is given a slanting cut while lower end is kept straight, 2/3rd portion of cutting is planted in the soil.

Sprouting of cuttings

Soon after planting the cuttings, they make contact with the soil and start growth. Leaves may dry up before the emergence of new leaves. Buds sprout and new leaves emerge. This may take 10-15 days depending on the kind of species and environment.

Raising plants in nursery beds

Young saplings being tender are not able to face the harsh climate and other difficult conditions in the field, so they are kept in the nursery for 5-6 months so that they are hardened or have taken enough growth to adjust and tolerate the field conditions.

After up-rooting from the seedbed, the young saplings are planted in well prepared and well manured nursery beds. The depth of planting is the same as was in the seedbed. Distance between two plants is kept 25-30 cm. These are kept in the nursery bed for 5-6 months or till they have attained sufficient height and growth and have trunk diameter of 1 cm. These are kept single stemmed. During this period, they are looked-after properly by keeping full vigil over plant protection, irrigation and nutritional needs.

Irrigation

Young saplings are provided irrigation after a week or so during summer and after 10 days during winter. These should not suffer dry conditions as once they are forced to drought, they do not recover. During monsoon rains, irrigation may be withheld and drainage may be needed. Avoid too much moisture or dryness around the root zone of seedlings/saplings/young plants.

Weeding

It is better to take out the weeds and other unwanted plants form the seedbed and nursery-bed as they rob the nutrition meant for sapling and compete for moisture, sunlight and other conditions of growth of the saplings. 15-16 weedings, in a year may be sufficient. During weeding, light hoeing may be done so that the root zone gets proper aeration which is useful for better growth of the plant and the micro-organisms living in the soil.

Propagation

Fruit trees are generally raised by seeds or cuttings which forms a stock. Since the plant so raised are not uniform in vigour and other fruiting characteristics, they are budded or grafted with desired scions and these plants exhibit uniform growth and fruiting behaviour.

Seedlings of 1 cm diameter, about 50 cm tall and single stemmed are budded or grafted in the proper season when their cell-sap is to start moving in the plant body. There are different methods of budding and grafting. T budding and Tongue grafting are most common. This may be done about 25-30 cm above the ground level. The union is tied over by a tape or an alkathene strip which is removed when the graft or the bud has taken up growth. It takes about a fortnight or so under normal conditions.

Later, the shoots arising out of the stock (potion of stem below budded or grafted place) are rubbed-off and the main stem is kept straight. If needed, support may be given.

Uprooting saplings

When the saplings have attained the requisite height and proper vigour, they are uprooted from the beds. Before uprooting, light irrigation, if possible may be given or wait for rains. Do not uproot when the soil is dry as this injures the roots.

From a moist soil, the plants are dug by a spade or a tiller and then lifted with care. When roots are needed to be covered with soil, as in case of evergreen trees, earth-ball should be dug carefully, taking precautions, that roots are not injured at all and the earth-ball remains a single unit.

Deciduous trees may be kept with bare roots. They may be bundled in 10's or so. After uprooting keep them under shade and then transport if necessary. Avoid exposure to direct sunlight and dry winds.

Movement of saplings

In case, the saplings are to be transported i.e., taken to a place which is away from the nursery or the plants are to be kept for few days before transplanting, they should be kept under shade and in a moist place.

Plants with earth-balls are wrapped in wet gunny bags or packed in polythene bags keeping their tops out and are kept moist. Sprinkling of water may be done twice a day during summer. Over-watering should be avoided as it leads to spoilage of earth-balls and favours fungal infection. Loading and unloading should be done with great care.

Deciduous plants i.e. those without leaves and with bare roots are also kept in a gunny bag by keeping them tied in a bundle. This bundle may be moistened on alternate day.

No injury to plants should be made during uprooting, transport or movement. It is better to pack them in convenient packs. Labelling may be done properly.

Young trees, seedlings raised by seeds or by cutting, or grafted plants are raised in a nursery and when these plants have attained the age of one year, they are uprooted and transplanted. Generally at this time, these plants are of single stem with a diameter of 1 cm or pencil thickness, height may be 60-70 cm and spread of the roots about 20 cm and length of the roots being 25-30 cm. Deciduous trees do not have leaves while evergreen trees have leaves.

Preparing a plant

On getting a plant from the nursery, it must be examined thoroughly. The leaves, stem and roots should be intact and not broken. They should be free from the attack of insects, pests and diseases.

Since the plant has been uprooted from the nursery and the nurseries are usually away from the place of planting, young plants should be kept under shade for few hours before being transplanted. During this period, they may be watered gently, if possible. Their earthballs should be intact and not broken or cracked. Cracked earthballs usually have damaged roots. Evergreen trees have earthballs while deciduous trees are taken without earth i.e., they are bare.

If the bare roots of the plants are broken or damaged, they may be pruned gently. It is advisable to dip the roots of plants in a fungicide solution for 5 minutes so that the remains of fungus on them die and then if they come across any fungal contamination in the soil, where they are transplanted, these treated plants will be able to tolerate the attack of fungus.

In case of evergreen trees, dried and damaged leaves may be removed gently. The wrap of gunny bag or leaves of banana may be removed at the time of transplanting only. Deciduous plants may be headed back if needed. For tall growing trees, it is necessary.

Watch carefully, the place of budding or grafting. It is necessary for fruit trees. It should be atleast 25 cm above the ground level and should be sound and healthy at the time of transplanting. Plant should be healthy and vigorous.

Preparing a place

When seedlings are transplanted in the field or elsewhere, they are supposed to get proper place for their establishment and later development. Therefore, this place should be sufficient for the roots to have anchorage and then develop in the years to come. Moreover, roots should be able to get proper and requisite nutrition from this place. In most of the cases, pits are prepared to place the plants. In other cases, the soil is pulverised or dug equal to the spread of roots of the would be plants, to have place for their establishment.

For *in situ* plantation, pits are prepared in the same manner as for transplanting.

Season of transplanting

Generally, there are two seasons for transplanting, i.e. monsoon and winter. During the monsoon season, mostly evergreen trees are planted. Usually, it is the rainy season, so plants do get sufficient amount of moisture for settling the roots and getting in contact with the soil particles. Similar situation is there during winter. In winter, there are less rains but on the contrary due to low temperature, there is less evaporation of water from the soil surface and less transpiration from the plant.

During winter, deciduous trees are transplanted. They are mostly in their dormant or rest stage and are leafless. So transpire less and are able to establish themselves.

If irrigation facilities are available and one can look-after the transplanted trees, he can transplant them as and when needed. This needs lot of care in transplanting and the establishment of the young plants.

Method of transplanting

Soil equal to the size of earthball or the spread of the roots of the plant, is removed from the centre of the pit to make sufficient place for the plant. Generally, this place has been marked by a wooden peg while filling the pit. In case, the pit has not been prepared earlier, soil equal to the size of the earthball, say about 30 cm deep and 30 cm wide is dug with the help of a spade.

The plant is placed in the centre of the dug place. Plant should be kept straight and held in one hand while the soil dug from the pit is placed around the root zone of the transplanted plant. When whole of the dug soil has been placed, it may be pressed gently so that the roots get direct contact with the soil. The pressing may be done by feet or with back of spade. The pressing is done to remove excess of air from the soil. It is better to make the surface doam shaped i.e., the slope should be outward, from trunk to outward.

In case of grafted or budded trees, one must observe that the union is well above the ground level. The level of the plant should be the same as was in the nursery, which can be ascertained by viewing the colour of the stem. Both the portions of the stem i.e., within the soil and outside the soil, have different colours.

If possible, light irrigation with a sprinkler may be given soon after transplanting.

Aftercare

A transplanted tree may show signs of wilting for a day or so since it needs some period to get established. As soon as the roots come in contact with the moist soil, they are activated. They swell and move further in search of water as a result the solutes from soil move into the plant and the plant starts functioning in a normal way. So due care has to be taken during this period. If the soil is not moist at the time of transplanting, light irrigation is a must. During summer, irrigation after 3 days is must but during winter, a weekly irrigation may suffice. The amount of water needed and the intervals between two irrigations will depend upon the moisture present in the soil, moisture needed by the plant and prevailing climatic conditions.

The first visible sign of successful transplanting is the regaining of turgidity by the plant which is evident from the stiffness of the leaves and the stem in case of evergreen trees while sprouting of young buds or leaves in case of deciduous trees.

CANOPY MANAGEMENT

When the trees are provided with congenial conditions of growth under suitable agro-climatic conditions, they start their growth in a manner which is usually the characteristics of a particular species. They may grow upward or sideways depending upon the environmental conditions. Thus, there is a need to have trees of good vigour having maximum growth so that they fulfil the purpose of their planting and as such one has to pay attention to their canopy.

Shape/Form Maintenance

Mostly trees have oval, oblong or round canopy but due to

sunlight and competition with other trees and their own branches, they may attain unwanted or irregular shape. For landscape, trees must confer to the design while for fruit production, trees should have more of reproductive growth to get good number of quality fruits. In case of forest trees, whether for timber or fuel, they need more of vegetative growth.

Sometimes, the trees are trained to have special type of canopy by having branches at desired places. This shape may be a bush, pillar, cordon, espalier, columnar, etc. For such shapes, the branches are trained and pruned in a special way. They may have to be bent by tying them down or forcing them to grow upright. Careful training and pruning is the answer to this. One may consult a book or an expert for this aspect.

In general, unwanted branches, which are intermingling with each other or are growing upright may be removed. Water shoots need to be removed from their bases while other shoots are pruned in such a way that there is a bud to grow. Big branches are lopped very carefully by giving a first lower cut and then a cut on the upper side. Wounds caused due to pruning or otherwise need to be dressed with Bordeaux paste or Chaubattia paste. No stubs should be left on the tree.

Removal of branches, shoots, etc., should be carried out when trees are either in dormancy or having very slow growth. Avoid pruning in summer and monsoon, as during this period, there is maximum danger of attack of pathogens.

Diseased and insect-infested parts may be removed as and when seen. If the cut is more than a cm in diameter, it must be smeared with a fungicide paste and the rest of the tree may be sprayed with a fungicide.

Main aim of canopy management is to provide a tree good framework that can have manageable number of branches and shoots for maximum output.

Plant Protection

Trees being living organisms are attacked by a number of pathogens like insects, fungus, bacteria and viruses. Tender plants are the easy targets of their attack.

Different types of insects like borers, caterpillars, thrips, scales, aphids, weevils, beetles, etc., affect different parts of the trees at various times. On seeing their attack, proper control measures are needed to be adopted.

Common fungal diseases are rust, root rot, stem rot, collar rot, canker, scab, moulds, powdery mildew, downy mildew, blight, blotches, fruit rot, etc. They may be controlled as soon as their symptoms or damage on trees is seen.

Bacteria and virus are other common pathogens. Bacterial canker, Gummosis, Mottling of leaves, etc., are quite common.

All these pathogens including the insect-pests, can be kept under control by mechanical and chemical means of control. Exposing the fungal spores and other parts, larvae, eggs, nymphs, etc., to sun by tilling the soil is easiest. Soil borne diseases and insects in the soil are controlled through this way as these are picked by birds when exposed on the surface and some are destroyed or inactivated by the sun-light, high temperature and exposure to air. Insects can be hand-picked or controlled by traps of various kinds. Fungicides and insecticides when sprayed on trees in the correct concentration at the right time do control the spread and check the population. Seed treatment is very useful against soil or seed borne diseases.

Apart from these, birds, monkeys, jackals, bears, pigs, etc., damage the trees. Suitable control measures must be adopted to avoid their attack.

While using the chemical method of control, one should be sure of the chemical, its concentration, time of application as suited to the maximum kill of the pathogen. Fruits or other edible portions should not be used atleast for 7 days after the spray.

There is biological method of control, which consists in allowing the predator insects to multiply to out-number the host parasite. One has to maintain the balance between host and parasite which is difficult for an ordinary grower.

Physical methods coupled with chemical methods are most suitable and successful in combating the major insects, pests and diseases.

Mineral Nutrition

Sometimes, trees may show symptoms of weak growth, abnormal size and colour of leaves, pre-mature leaf fall or fruit fall, scorching of leaves and twigs, etc. These symptoms are generally due to lack of minerals in the soil. It has been observed that in many orchards and other plantations, there is deficiency of boron, zinc, manganese and calcium in some patches. These can be corrected with the application of the desired salt of the mineral, may be to the soil or on the foliage. Soil application is expensive and takes a long time to make-up the deficiency while foliage application is quick and can be repeated if the first spray has not shown good response.

One should consult an expert for identification of the symptoms of a particular mineral element before start of the spray. For general use, Urea @1.0 per cent may be sprayed on the foliage to get lush green leaves of good shape and size.

As a general practice, annual dose of manures and fertilizers should be applied. Farm Yard manure must be well rotten otherwise there is danger of attack of white ants. One must add an ample quantity of the natural organic manure to the soil so that artificial fertilizer can be used by the plants. Farm Yard Manure, Compost, Green Manure, different types of oil cakes, etc., form the basic organic matter of the soil. They are essential both for the tree and the micro-organisms living in the soil.

Aftercare

Trees are transplanted in well-prepared pits or are raised *in situ* in well prepared trenches. At the time of transplanting, there should be enough moisture in the soil so that the roots of the transplanted tree can make immediate and easy contact with the soil particles of the pit. In case, there is less moisture, •transplanting should immediately be followed by irrigation. One or two trees can be irrigated by a watering can but on large scale, one has to irrigate them with a suitable method.

Keep the tree straight as far as possible. They can be staked if necessary but stakes should not overpower or over-shadow the main plant. Stakes should be removed as soon as the trunk has started growth in the proper direction.

Hoeing and weeding are a must as these operations open up the soil for aeration and make the soil pulverised to absorb moisture. Weeds are also destroyed either by cutting them to the ground level or uprooting them from the soil. Basins or trenches should preferably be kept clean of weeds. Weeds are competitors with the main trees for all its requirements. It has been observed in many cases, that weeds grow in a better way than the main tree due to neglect or carelessness. Light hoeing should be done to avoid injury to roots.

Plant protection measures are to be adopted as and when felt necessary. One may consult the entomologist or a pathologist for this purpose. It is better to follow the recommended package of practices for raising of a specie. As soon as the symptoms of attack of a parasite or a pathogen are visible, due care should be taken. If the attack is of minor incidence, i.e. less than 5%, hand picking or cultural method of control may be adopted but when there is severity of damage, chemical means of control must be adopted. Strict precautions should be followed while adopting the chemical control measures.

Removal of insect-infested and disease-affected twigs, buds, branches, fruits, etc., should be carried out as and when observed. Cuts more than a cm in diameter must be smeared with a fungicide paste like Chaubattia Paste or Bordeaux Paste and suitable fungicide solution may be sprayed on whole of the tree to cover other wounds.

Training and pruning are also needed to maintain the tree shape and to keep it in a good state of growth. Over-crowding and unwanted shoots may be removed. A careful watch may be essential to rub-off the unwanted growth of tender portions. The tree must get proper aeration and sunlight to have luxuriant growth.

The tree is to be maintained in its proper shape, free from diseases and insects and in healthy condition.

5
CHAPTER

TREES IN RELATION TO ENVIRONMENT

Trees are an integral part of the environment. Our environment has polluted to such an extent that it is now very hard to live in this condition. In big cities, one feels congested and oppressed by the pollution of air, soil, water, noise, etc. Following are some of the salient causes responsible for this:

I. PRESSURE ON FORESTS

Forests include the trees, bushes, trailing plants and soil covering plants. Big trees provide shade and shelter to other plants while the remaining three types of plants protect the soil from being denuded or eroded away by rain or wind. Man has exploited the forests for all kinds of materials like wood, coal, timber, medicines, etc., some of the forests have been cut away or removed for sake of money.

In order to earn revenue, large areas of forests are being removed in many states that has lessened the area under forests. The removal of trees has threatened the lives of many organisms dependent upon them chiefly, the wild animals, plants and human beings. Wild animals are the ones that keep a balance between themselves through their natural means. Due to their presence in the jungle, they protect the trees (forests) from the reach of human beings. Some of the species are now under the category of endangered species. One may have to see them in zoos or museums.

Plant species too have become endangered. Many of them are already out of scene. Others are following. The major reason of their extinction is soil erosion due to removal of soil cover from the land. All plants are essential for the energy reservoir of the world. In fact, these are the laboratories where the solar energy is converted into potential energy through photosynthesis from the carbon dioxide and water received from the environment. First stable product formed is carbohydrate, which is a basis of all the organic compounds in the world. Their saturated form is fat. When nitrogen is combined with them, they become proteins, enzymes, vitamins, growth hormones and many other compounds, which are directly needed by the human beings and animals. Petrol, kerosene, coal, gems, etc. are products of the plant origin.

Due to depletion of forest wealth, the land surface becomes free of the vegetative cover. The soil cover is exposed to vagaries of nature like wind, water and sun, all combine to show their effects which ends in the shifting away of the cover of soil from the top of the soil. In fact, this layer has formed after millions of years of decomposition and disintegration of the organic matter and mineral matter of the rocks. This is the most fertile cover that is sufficient for the growth of plants over the surface. The shift of this cover causes loss to the surface from where it has been removed and then it causes loss to the place where it deposits. Being soluble in water, it goes to the sea without being utilized or trapped in between.

Thus, the pressure of forests is one of the most potent factors responsible for loss of energy and not-receipt of many useful products form the forests. One should always keep in mind that the forests are the trees and other plants that are being left to grow themselves without the intervention of the mankind. Forests do have their own world.

2. INDUSTRIALIZATION

As a mark of development progress, it is believed that industrial countries are doing better than others. In facts, it has become a symbol of progress or synonym to progress in the eyes of few economists and planners. This is one side of the picture in which by providing an industry in as area, natural resources are harnessed to the maximum level, people get employment and this leads to prosperity of the inhabitants. Theoretically, it is correct but when it taken practically, there is exploitation of natural resources to the maximum extent without caring for the future. Further, though people get employment but they leave their own traditional profession and the land which was under crops or other uses has been brought under an industry and the people have to work in the industry/factory.

In factories, most of the workers are skilled or semi-skilled workers who are usually brought or recruited from other areas. Local people get only a small chance of work. The factories or industries are set to provide alternative employment or jobs to the local inhabitants but they rarely get the jobs. Ultimately, the prosperity of the local people remains at the same level and this is bound to increase through other means that is the indirect impact of industrialization.

Provision of huge infrastructure, particularly for large industries, has another problem for the area. These structures have a damaging effect on the land. The vibrations produced while installing or constructing cause tremendous loss to the ecology. Once they start functioning and come in production, many types of gases are emitted which are usually harmful for the flora, fauna and other living beings. Then, there is discharge of unwanted materials from these industries. Since it can not be used for useful purposes, it is thrown as a waste product that flows over the adjoining areas or is made to go into a channel of water or a river. Both these by-products are harmful for the human beings. They lead to number of diseases that may be incurable. Asthma, bronchitis, etc. are such common diseases.

3. INDISCRIMINATE USE OF NATURAL RESOURCES

Land is a reservoir of natural resources to the maximum level. Many products like petrol, coal, gems, gold, copper, zinc, manganese, mica, iron, etc. are received from the mother earth. For our use we are exploiting the earth. Simple and popular case is of limestone. This stone is being taken from the rocks or ore for various means in which number of diggings and blasting are done which damage the rock and vegetation. Further, when it has been dug, there is a fall of the remaining rock and some layer of earth is thrown away which is affected by wind and water. This causes soil erosion and shifting of land from one place to another leading to loss of fertility of the soil and eco-imbalance. Likewise, there are plenty of stone quarries in the country. Gold and other metals when extracted have to be purified by chemical and physical processes that are intricate and cause huge loss to the vegetation and to the topography of the soil and earth. It also hampers the activities of the micro-fauna present in the land.

4. SOCIO-CULTURAL ISSUES

Man is a social animal and needs company of others, may be of plants, animals and human beings. All are to live in a compromising atmosphere. With the development in all fields, the nature, habits, customs and social structure of the society has undergone a severe change. In the past, villagers were dependent upon the forest for their day-to-day demand of firewood, timber, food, medicines and fodder for cattle and other animals. With the depletion of forests, they have no choice for fuel-wood except either to cut the trees or to adopt some other measures. For fuel, everybody does not have the reach for cooking gas and like facilities and the solar system of cooking. In hilly areas, particularly, in the higher hills, where the temperature goes minus 200°C or son in winter, people have to keep them warm which is only possible through firewood. Solar and electric energy can not compete with this due to lack of sunshine and less supply or erratic electric supply, respectively. Further, people have acquired the habit of living in houses having woodwork inside to keep the room warm in winter and cool in summer. It is estimated that wood paneling a room may cost about Rs. 20,000 or so. It is due to high price and great demand of wood.

Due to change in the habit of residential facilities, people look for good and capacious houses, which are being built on the land that was meant for cultivation of crops. With the increase in population, there is bound to be an increase in the demand of residences, schools and other public utility services. More roads, railway lines, paths, parks, community halls, etc. have to be provided to meet the requirement of the public. Some of the good areas have already been engulfed by the heavy industries and then much is being utilized by the constructing such buildings at places which are not productive, barren, and rocky or wastelands.

The living standards of people have improved. Nobody wants to enjoy the old-traditional houses. They want palatial house with modern facilities but they do not care for the waste being thrown out of their houses. Lot of garbage, particularly of metallic nature like tin and plastic is thrown out as a waste product. Both are not easily degradable. Tin and other metals may take many centuries to be converted into useful purpose but the plastic is hazardous for nature and human beings. Losses caused by plastic are plugging of channels, danger of its catching fire, etc. They pose a problem for the eco-system of the earth. Until and unless the use of metal and plastic is not curbed, other methods employed to check the pollution of environment may go waste or less productive.

5. ECONOMICAL ISSUES

Our society has three types of people: rich, middle class and poor people. The income if a family has a direct bearing on the spread and control of pollution. Highly rich people have plenty of money and resources to dispose-off the waste products form their dwelling but where it is done, is another story. They try to clean or get their surroundings clean but spoil the atmosphere of others. Poor people have no resources, even to meet their primary demands. They throw away the litter etc. wherever they want since their dwellings are unwarranted. Some of them have forcibly occupied the areas for example, on both sides of the rail track and water channels. These people do not have enough resources and awareness to keep the surroundings clean. The main reason being lack of financial resources. Middle class people have the awareness but not the time to devote for carrying out projects for keeping the environment clean.

Enough money, will power, determination and hard labour is required to maintain rather than to improve the fragile ecosystem which has been made a mere skeleton and denuded and most of the hills adjoining to the valley areas have been eroded.

6. IMPACT OF POLLUTION

The pollution in the environment is visible in all spheres.

Water, which we use in many ways, is polluted by various sources. It has become a den of diseases. Many diseases develop and multiply due to bad sanitation and impure water. Water is the carrier of many diseases, viruses, bacteria and insects.

Air, we breathe is also polluted by various gases which are emitted by the waste of the industries, houses, factories and other dwellings in cities and big towns. The amount of permissible pollutants has long been crossed. At some places, the air when saturated with fumes of various gases, particularly from the vehicles is irritant to the eyes and harmful to lungs. People have to go for gas masks for getting clean air.

Land has been accumulated with many impurities that have come from the waste of industries, dumping of animal carcasses, partial decay of organic matter, plastic and metallic deposits, soil erosion, loss of bio-mass of the soil, restricted or arrested activities of the micro-flora and micro-fauna, indiscriminate use of pesticides and other chemicals, etc. The natural topography of the land has been completely distributed and fertility has deteriorated. Huge area has been converted into deserts and wastelands.

Above all, there is noise pollution. The noise produced by factories, vehicles and working of various machines have led to impairing of hearing by human beings. When the noise is around 20-30 decibels, it is considered normal but when this exceeds this limit it causes huge losses. Tractor and heavy machinery produces a noise of 95 to 140 decibels that is harmful for growth of plants. This is also harmful for the animals and human beings.

All these factors have a direct effect on the human beings, animals and plants. Rainfall, temperature, wind, hails, soil conditions, sunlight availability, atmospheric changes, pollutants, diseases, thunderstorms, etc. affect the environment to a large extent. This pollution has to be checked by all means so that we can have a clean atmosphere to live.

7. CONSERVATION

There is an urgent need to conserve the ecosystem so as to have an healthy environment for better living of all creatures. There are two ways; to check the pollution and then to improve the already degraded environment. If we are able to adopt the first step in the real sense, the degraded environment will be automatically on the improvement. For this, we have to create awareness among ourselves about the measures to be adopted for combating the problem of environmental degradation that includes soil erosion, depletion of forest wealth, scarcity of forest-based raw materials and many hardships to the people in terms of food, fuel, fodder, water and other resources for which we depend directly on land and forests.

The only way to conserve is by means of planting vegetation to provide a green cover to the earth surface. As has been proposed, 50-60 percent of the geographical area of the country is to be brought under green cover, particularly in the hilly area but at present, only 15-20 per cent area is under the green cover. This includes all the crops that have already been planted like annual and perennial plants.

Green cover is of vegetation that provides us the natural sources of energy, apart from other benefits. Plants kingdom is the only laboratory of nature where the solar energy of sun is converted into the most valuable energy to meet all the demands of the human beings. The green colour of plant kingdom is due to chlorophyll that has the capability of converting the solar energy for our use. Carbon-dioxide from the environment and water from the soil is converted into carbohydrates that yield to the formation of other organic compounds like fats, proteins, enzymes, hormones, wood, petrol and many other products of our daily use as food and other utilities. Above all, the green cover that is organic in nature has the capacity to absorb and neutralize the harmful and toxic effects of soil, air, water and noise pollutions.

Trees are best suited for the purpose of protection of soil, water and air from pollution by providing the green cover. They provide space and shade for the prosperity and proper functioning of the shrubs, bushes, climbers, creepers and all sorts of vegetation under their canopy. They check soil erosion and conserve soil moisture. They purify the atmosphere through exchange and neutralization of harmful gases. Trees have the ability to conserve solar energy into radiant energy through photosynthesis. There is proper utilization of the land and other natural resources that improves the soil conditions and the environment. By increasing the biomass, local climate, micro-flora and micro-fauna are able to provide much respite in the maintenance of eco-system.

6
CHAPTER

DESCRIPTION OF TREES

SILVER FIR

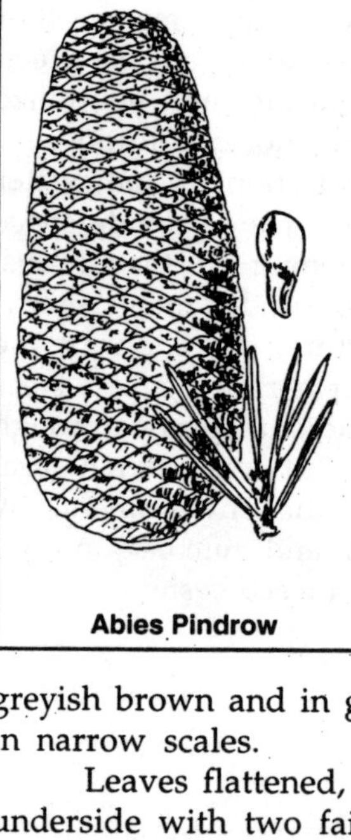

Abies Pindrow

It is a tree of temperate region but is found growing satisfactorily in the sub-tropical region of this part of the country, particularly in the Himalayan tract between 2500 m to 3600 m above mean sea level in almost all the hill areas. Trees are also found at lower elevations under cool and moist conditions. These are mostly found in shady places on northern slopes.

In vernacular, it is known is Tosh. *Abies pindrow* Spach is the botanical name and Family is *Pinaceae Coniferae.*

Trees are evergreen in nature, tall about 50-60 m, and resemble the Cupruss tree in its outline. Trunk is cylindrical with dark foliaged crown. Bark is smooth on young branches and greyish brown and in grown up trees, it may have deep vertical grooves in narrow scales.

Leaves flattened, linear, stiff, 5-7 cm long, apex with 2 sharp teeth, underside with two faint silvery lines on either side of the raised mid-rid, upper side is dark green and shining.

Male and female cones appear on same tree. Male catkins are axillary, sessile, clustered, 2 cm across, appear in April. Female cones are terminal, cylindrical, solitary or in distinct pairs, borne erect on horizontal branches, ovoid. Mature cones are ovoid, 10-15 cm long and 4-6 cm in diameter, dark purple when ripe, scales thin, slightly thickened along the rounded margins between which the points of the bracts just appear. They ripen in September-October.

Seeds are winged, broad, round and about 2 to 3.5 cm long.

Mature wood is white to dull brownish white and is used for packing cases, tea chests, fuel, timber, etc., since it is soft, light and not very durable. Pulp is used for paper manufacture.

Abies Spectabilis

HIMALAYAN SILVER FIR

It is another kind of Silver Fir, tree which is found growing from Afghanistan to Bhutan in the hilly areas which span all the States falling under the North-Western Himalaya. It is seen in forests between the elevations of 2800 m to 4000 m above mean sea level.

Botanical name of the tree is *Abies spectabilis* (D. Don.) Spach and belongs to Family *Coniferae/Pinaceae.*

Tree are evergreen in nature but shedding of leaves is regular and new leaves take the place of older leaves.

Trees are slender, pyramidial, going as high as 20-30 m. Bark is dark grey, deeply longitudinally grooved. Young branchlets or branches are hairy but soon become hairless while upper branches are horizontal.

Leaves are green, shining, distinctly parted on the upper side of the branchlets and point sideways and with the apex of the leaf rounded and notched. Flattened, 2.5 cm to 7.5 cm long, pale beneath with incurved margins.

Male and female flowers appear. Male catkins are cylindrical and 5 cm long.

Fruits are known as cones, which are formed from the female flowers. They are dark purple in colour, erect, cylindrical, 10-20 cm x 4-7.5 cm. Cones are seen only in the upper tree zone during April-May and they ripen in September-October.

Wood of the tree is used for building purposes and roof shingles. Trees provide quality timber. Cones are used as fuel. Leaves are used for preparation of decoction used against bronchitis and pulmonary infections.

Acacia arabica

KIKAR

It is an evergreen tree found abundantly in the moist tropical region and is extensively found growing in the lower hills where the climate is bit mild. Under the outer Himalayas, the trees are found in the lower hills of Himachal Pradesh in Paonta, Nalagarh, Bilaspur while in Uttaranchal in Dehradun and lower areas of the Kumaon region. In Jammu and Kashmir, trees are seen growing on wastelands and drier slopes. It is quite common in Punjab and Haryana.

Botanically it is known as *Acacia arabica* Wild. belonging to genus *Acacia* and Family *Mimosaceae*. Trees are moderately tall, about 8 m with a spread of 6-7 m and with umbrella like canopy. Main trunk may be 60-75 cm in diameter. Bark is greyish brown to dark brown nearly black in colour and scaly in nature which peels off to give space for the new bark.

Leaves are compound, small leaflets, green, borne with petioles; stipules, spiny and straight, white and very long on old branches. Leaflets are 20-40 in a single leaf.

Flowers are mostly yellowish which appear in bunches during rainy season. These are small, fragrant but conspicuous in shape.

Pods are strap like, green when fresh but turns brown and become hard on maturity. There are 5-10 seeds in each pod, separated by contracting of pod sheath in between two seeds. Seeds are circular, 0.5x0.5 cm and brown in colour.

It is a partial shade giving tree whose twigs are used as tooth brushes and fuel. Leaves along with twigs are used for feeding animals, particularly the goats. Wood is used for many purposes both in domestic and commercial. It is hard, heavy and durable.

Pods have medicinal value and are also used for tanning. Gum is also extracted which is used for pasting or eating. It is a good tree for road side plantation and for development of wastelands and grasslands as it enhances the soil fertility through its roots which are nodulated where nitrogen fixing bacteria synthesize the proteins by using the atmospheric nitrogen.

Acacia catechu

KHAIR

A commercial tree of warm and dry region is found predominantly in the forests in Shivalik hills, parts of the hills of Uttaranchal to Kashmir valley in the altitudinal range of 400-1000 m but mostly 500-800 m above mean sea level. Rains in the range of 50-200 cm are sufficient for better growth of trees. In Himachal Pradesh, trees are found in Bilaspur, Nahan, Hamirpur, Una, Kangra, Dalhousie, Solan and Kunihar areas. In other States, trees are found scattered in the lower valley areas.

It is a moderately sized tree about 10-12 cm tall, which is deciduous in nature. Botanical name is *Acacia catechu* Willd. and belongs to Family *Mimosaceae*.

Tree has a light feathery crown and the trunk has coloured bark dark grey that peels off in long strips.

Branches are hairy, thorny and brown.

Leaves are shining, 7-10 cm long with scattered prickles, pinnae in pairs of 10-20 leaflets, linear, glabrous and green.

Pale yellow flowers appear in cylindrical spikes in May-June.

Pods are flat thin, brown, shining with 5-6 seeds in each pod. They ripen during winter (October-December).

Seeds are dark greenish, smooth, shining and about 5 mm in diameter.

Katha and cutch are prepared from the heart-wood of the tree, which is used in medicines and other preparations. Heartwood yields brown khaki dye. It provides a valuable timber; outer wood is used for Katha. Leaves are fed to cattle. They contain 13-18 per cent crude protein, 21 per cent crude fibre, 2.0 per cent calcium and 0.1 per cent phosphorus.

PHALAHI

Trees are fairly spread in the dry to moist tropical climate in the sub-Himalayan tract and the outer Himalayas from Jammu westwards. They are abundantly found in the lower hills, valleys and sub-mountain areas also. They are best upto 1300 m above mean sea level.

It belongs to Family *Mimosaceae* and its botanical name is *Acacia modesta* Wall. Sometimes trees are also known by the name of Phulai or Phulahi.

Trees are evergreen in nature and may attain the height of 7-8 m with a spread of 5-6 m. It is a thorny tree with drooping branches to provide umbrella shape to its canopy. Bark is dark brown, rough and with irregular cracks.

Leaves are green with grey tinge, hairy, stipules soon fall off, 6-10 leaflets, obovate.

Flowers are white to pale yellowish in colour, which appear in summer, small but clustered.

Pods are 5-7 cm x 0.5 cm, flat or coiled, hairy, oblong, dirty grey to green in colour with a stalk of about 0.5 cm length.

Leaves of the tree are used for feeding animals; tender twigs are used as tooth brushes. Wood is hard and durable and is used for preparation of agricultural tools and implements, cart wheels and fuel. It is a good soil-binding tree, and is drought resistant, so suitable for wastelands and marginal lands.

Acer Caesium

TREKHAN

Trees are found growing in forests and open grassy places in the Himalayas from Afghanistan to central Nepal, in the altitudinal range of 2200-3300 m above mean sea level.

Acer caesium Wall. is a fairly large tree often going upto 25 m in height with a girth of 2-3 m.

Trees belong to Family *Aceraceae* and is deciduous in nature. Trees are fairly large with thin grey bark.

Leaves are large, 8-15 cm long, broader than long with a heart-shaped base and with 5 unequal broad and long-pointed coarsely saw-toothed lobes. Leaves are usually pale and glaucous beneath but red when young.

Flowers are greenish white or yellow, 5 mm across, which appear with the young leaves in branched flat-topped clusters during December/March-April.

Fruits have wings, which may be divergent or sometimes overlapping. Nuts are dark brown with a hump like swelling.

Wood is of good quality and is used for carving, making bowls, plates and ladles. It is also suitable for making of furniture, frames, boards, etc.

Acee oblongum

PAGOI

The tree is also known by the name of Pandag in Hindi in Himachal Pradesh. They are spread in the altitudinal range between 700-2000 m above mean sea level in the lower and mid-hills of temperate Himalaya, right from Pakistan to China. In Uttaranchal, it is found in shady places between 1500-2000 m above mean sea level.

Botanical Name is *Acer oblongum* Wall. and it belongs to the Family *Aceraceae.*

Tree is evergreen in nature.

Leaves are glabrous, not lobed, oblong, 7-12 cm x 2-5 cm, entire, long, pointed, upper surface dark green while lower one is whitish green.

Flowers are greenish white that appear during February-April in hairy corymbs.

Fruit is hairless with wings narrowed to the base placed either parallel or widely divergent or almost horizontal.

Wood is soft and is used for manufacture of sports goods.

Leaves are lopped for fodder. It is a fast growing tree.

Achras Zapota

SAPOTA

It is a common fruit tree of the tropical region which is found growing in all the southern States and central India.

Sapota or sapodilla is an evergreen tree which belongs to Family *Sapotaceae* and the botanical name is *Achras zapota*, syn. *Manilkara Zapota* L.

Trees are of medium size going 10-12 m in height and 6 m in spread. These are deep-rooted and have upright branching with a strong trunk having thick bark of dark brown colour. Generally, the trunk is straight upto 75 cm from the ground level. Canopy is oval.

Leaves are green, lanceolate, pointed, 10x5 cm, glossy on upper surface and slightly rough underneath, petioled and look like that of mango.

Flowers are solitary and axillary but sometimes clustered.

Fruits are round to oval or egg-shaped, potato coloured, skin rough but thin and not edible, 5-8 cm across. Pulp is light brown, soft, juicy and sweet.

Seeds are dark brown which look like blackish brown, hard, flat, shining, oblong and pointed on one side, 1.5-2 cm long and 0.5 cm wide. There are 2-3 seeds in each fruit, which are placed in the centre of the fruit in separate chambers.

Trees do not need pruning or training except to remove the unwanted branches.

100 g pulp of fruit contains 73.7 g moisture, 21.4 g carbohydrates, 1.1 g fat, 0.7 g protein, 0.5 g mineral matter, 2.6 g fibre, phosphorus 27 mg, iron 1.25 mg, magnesium 25 mg, calcium 28 mg, sodium 50 mg, potassium 269 mg, copper 0.08 mg, manganese 0.68 mg, zinc 0.16 mg, chromium 0.08 mg, sulphur 17 mg, chlorine 26 mg, Vita A 97 I.U., Thiamine 0.02 mg, Riboflavin 0.03 mg, Niacin 0.2 mg, Vita C 6 mg, and calorific value is 98 Kcal.

Adina Cordifolia

SAFFRON TEAK

Though it is found in the sub-Himalayan tract from Nepal eastwards to Assam in plenty but in western part, it is also common in deciduous forests. Its existence is seen up to 1000 m on slopes. Trees are of tropical and sub-tropical climate but are found in other tracts also.

It is also known as Harud or Haldu and belongs to Family *Rubiaceae*. Botanical name is *Adina cordifolia* Benth. and Hook.

Trees are tall and deciduous with a large crown and a straight fluted pole up to 15 m or so in height. Old trees are often buttressed. Bark is rough. Branches are horizontal and may be massive but when in plantation, there is a clean bole. Old leaves are shed before the mid of February and new ones appear in May-June, thus, the tree remains leafless from February to March or April. As the new leaves unfold, the large whitish stipules enclosing the leaf buds fall.

Leaves are cordate-orbicular or obovate, 10-15 cm in diameter, abruptly accuminate, pubescent beneath, petiole is 2-6 cm long, hairy with stipules.

Flower heads are yellow, appear in June-July.

Fruits are globose and ripen only in March.

Seeds are small.

Wood is durable and is used for many purposes like flooring making canoes, cigar boxes, toys, combs, agricultural implements, etc Bark is used as an antiseptic and in other medicinal uses. Juice is used to kill worms. Leaves are used as fodder.

Aegle Marmelos

GOLDEN APPLE

These are trees of religious and medicinal importance. Though the trees grow best under sub-tropical climate but are also found growing in plenty under lower hills and valley areas in western Himalayas but no attempt seems to have been made for their commercial plantation in any of the States in whole of the country.

Vernacular names for the tree are Bilwa, Bael, Bel patra, etc. and it belongs to Family *Rutaceae,* and botomical name is *Aegle marmelos* (L.) Corr.

The trees are tall (10-12 m) and spreading which provide shade and shelter. Trunk is strong with white greyish bark, which is furrowed and corky. Branches may be spiny, upright and strong. Canopy is oval to round.

Leaves are compound, of 3 leaflets, green, large and fleshy.

Flowers are greenish white, sweet smelling, which appear in clusters during spring or early summer.

Fruits are large, berry, round, hard, 6-8 cm thick stalked, filled with mucilaginous substance, which is sweet. These have woody shells.

Seeds are small, many, flat, oblong and placed in the aromatic mucilage.

Trees are multipurpose in nature, every part of it is valued. It is grown near temples since its fruits and leaves are used for worshipping, particularly, Lord Shiva. Other uses include the use of leaves as fodder, twigs as firewood, fruits for making medicines and syrups; gum is obtained from the stem, etc. Wood is very hard and durable. The trees are valued for both therapeutic and nutritional values.

Preparations from leaves and fruits are used in control over disorders like diarrhoea and dysentry. From the point of nutrition, 100 g of edible pulp contains 61.50 g moisture, 1.80 g protein, 0.30 g fat, 1.70 g minerals, 2.90 g fibre, 31.80 g carbohydrates, 85 mg calcium, 1861 I.U. Vita A, 0.13 mg, Thiamine 0.03 mg, Riboflavin 1.10 mg, Niacin 8 mg, Vita C 50 mg, phosphorus 0.6 mg, iron 600 mg, potassium 0.21 mg, copper and calorific value is 137 Kcal.

Aesculus Indica

HORSE CHEST NUT

Trees are mostly found in the moist sub-tropical climate but are also found in the temperate region where they are good as avenue, shade, landscape, road-side plantation and for folder, timber and food. They are widely spread between altitudinal range of 1800 m to 3000 m in North West Himalayas in Jammu and Kashmir, Himachal Pradesh and Uttaranchal.

Horse Chest Nut is known as Khanor, Kanor, Pangar or Kandar in Hindi. Its botanical name is *Aesculus indica* (Camb.) Hook and belongs to Family *Hippocastanaceae.*

Trees are deciduous in nature shedding their leaves during autumn and then new leaves emerge during spring reason. Trees are fairly large, i.e. both tall and spreading, may be 15-20 m tall with a spread of 15-30 m. Canopy is almost round. Branching is strong. Trunk is fairly thick and long. Bark is dark brown and smooth, which peels off in long narrow strips.

Leaves are compound, long (10-15 cm), long petiolated with 5-9 leaflets, tapering towards their free ends, glabrous, green and opposite, elliptical, sharply toothed and 15-25 cm long. Flowers are white and borne in bunches on 15 to 30 cm long panicles in spring or early summer.

Fruits are nuts enclosed in a fuzzy covering of Khaki (brown) colour. Nuts are ovoid, dark brown, smooth, heart shaped, 2.5-5 cm across and each capsule has 1-3 large, dark brown and shining seeds.

Wood is highly durable and is used for furniture making and in building construction work. Also used as fuel wood. Leaves are fed to cattle in scarcity conditions. Bark is used as medicine and for preparation of insecticide. Nuts are eaten as a food after roasting.

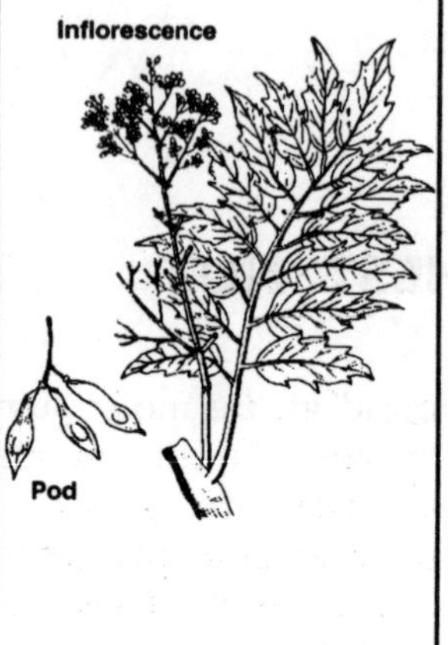

Ailanthus Excelsa

MAHARUKH

Trees are found growing on light or less fertile soil, i.e. the marginal lands in the sub-tropical climate under the altitudinal range of 2000 m above mean sea level where the annual rainfall is around 350 to 500 mm and can withstand snowfall. Valleys and lower hills having moist climate are best suited.

Botanical name is *Ailanthis excelsa* Roxb. and belongs to Family *Simarubaceae.*

Trees are tall about 25 m in height and deciduous in nature. Bark is usually of white or light grey colour. Trunk is stout and may be twisted or straight.

Leaves are compound in 6-12 pairs, opposite.

Flowers are of amber or light yellow colour, 8 mm diameter and in bunches. These appears in February-March.

Fruits red, are 4-6 cm long and 1.0 to 1.5 cm wide pods, which are flat and rounded on both ends. One seed in each pod.

Wood is usually light, soft and of white colour which is used for making of packing cases, floats, small boxes like match box and tea chests, toys, etc. Leaves are lopped for feeding goats.

Trees are used as shade and ornamental in general but they serve good purpose of soil conservation. It is fast growing tree which is good for wasteland development.

SIRAN

It is a tree of moist tropical and sub-tropical climate and is found growing on river sides and cultivated areas in the altitudinal range of 300-1300 m above sea level in the sub-Himalayan tract of Himalayan valleys. It is also common in Kangra valley in Himachal Pradesh.

Botanical name of tree is *Albizia chinensis* (Osbeck) Merr. and it belongs to the Family *Mimosaceae.*

Trees are deciduous in nature but may behave as evergreen in some parts. Canopy is broad and flat-topped, Bark is smooth with grey hairs. Stipules are 2-5 cm long.

Leaves are compound, green, 6-20 pairs of pinnate end and leaflets. Leaflets may be 6-10 cm long.

Yellowish white flowers with long white filaments sometimes tinged with purple colour appear from April to June when the tree is lush green with foliage.

Pods are pale reddish green when young and turn light brown on ripening during September to December. They are 8-15 cm long and 1.2 to 2.0 cm broad, flat, glabrous and wrinkled.

Seeds are long, flat, ovate, greenish brown and smooth. Pods rarely open on trees and can be seen hanging on trees even after three months of ripening.

It is a shade tree in tea gardens. Leaves may be fed to animals but continuous feeding leads to toxicity.

Albizza Lebbek Benth : Siris

EAST INDIAN WALNUT

Trees are found scattered in mixed deciduous forests in dry to wet tropical climates, ascending to 1300 m above mean sea level in the western part of Himalayas and the Shivalik ranges. It has become so common with planters that except the temperate region, it is found growing everywhere in the Himalayas and is common throughout the country.

It is generally known as Siris in this part of the country.

Siris is *Albizia lebbek* (L.) Benth. belonging to Family *Mimosaceae* so is able to fix the atmospheric nitrogen for use in the soil for other crops. It is a deciduous tree reaching to height of 12-20 m with a broad crown. Bark is pale and rough.

Leaves are compound, abruptly bipinnate, leaflets 6-18, 3x1 cm, elliptical, oblong and terminals are ovate-oblong, mid-rib is prominent and green.

Flowers are cream white to yellow, fragrant, on 5-8 cm long peduncles. They appear in April-May.

Fruits attain full size in about 3 months (August) and they (pods) remain green up to October. Ripe pods are flat, thin, straw coloured, 20-30 cm long and 3-5 cm broad.

Each pod has 6-12 seeds which are smooth, light brown, oblong or obvate, 0.7-1.2 x 0.6-0.9 cm with a hard testa.

Leaves are used as fodder as they provide excellent fodder having 30 per cent crude protein. Bark, leaves, flowers and seeds are used for preparation of various medicines of local use. Bark is used for tanning and preparation of local medicines. Wood is used for making furniture and other domestic articles and as fuel. Good avenue and roadside plantation tree which is good for soil conservation.

Alnus Nepalensis

ALDER

These trees are found growing in the altitudinal range of 1000-3000 m above mean sea level near the river sides, wet gullies, deep formations and on land-slips throughout the Himalayas from the Ravi River eastwards in Himachal Pradesh, Uttaranchal and parts of Kashmir. They are also found in Khasi Hills and adjoining areas.

In vernacular the trees are famous as Utis (Atis), Kunish, etc.

Botanical name of the tree is *Alnus nepalensis* Don, which belongs to the Family *Betulaceae.* It is an evergreen tree with a dark green bark, which becomes silvery grey in the open. Medium to large sized tree. Crown is spreading. Branches are mostly hairy.

Leaves are elliptic to ovate with rounded or shortly pointed apex, entire or with undulated margins, leaflets are in pairs of 10-18.

Inflorescence is catkin. Male catkins are 10-20 cm long, many and panicled. Cone is cylindrical, 1-3 cm long, small, woody bracts covering the crustaceous 1 seeded nut.

Nutlets (seeds) are with papery wings. Seeds ripen during winter.

In Himachal Pradesh, trees are lopped for fodder as a last resort for feeding cattle. Timber is of fair quality. Wood is soft and light and easily worked. Bark is used for dyeing and tanning. Good for soil conservation and wasteland development.

KUNISH

It as another common tree of *Alnus* spp. found growing in the Western Temperate Himalayas in the moist region in Giri Valley of Himachal Pradesh and like places in Uttaranchal and Kashmir Hills and till Western Nepal. Best are in 1800-2700 m above mean sea level in temperate to sub-tropical climate in Western Temperate Himalaya.

Botanical name is *Alnus nitida* (Spach) Endl. and this belongs to the Family *Betulaceae*. Vernacular common names are Kosh, Piyak, etc.

It is evergreen tree going 20 m high with dark brown or blackish shining bark. Bark becomes furrowed and rough on old trunks. Branchlets are hairy but twigs are usually hairless.

Leaves are long-pointed more or less distinctly toothed, lateral nerves 8-12 pairs, smooth beneath (lateral veins not reaching the margins).

Flowering is during September-October.

Male catkins are 5-10 cm long, in erect and sometimes racemes. Female cones mostly solitary, axillary, and are 1-2 cm long.

Fruiting cones are 2 to 4 cm across, solitary or 2-5 in short, erect racemes.

Wings of nutlet are thick and leathery.

Leaves are lopped for fodder, which is used for feeding cattle and goats. Fuel wood quality is also good. Timber is used for making furniture, packing cases, etc. Bark is used for dyeing and tanning.

Anacardium Occidentale

CASHEW NUT

Trees are valued for their nutty seeds and fruits, which are grown near the coastal areas around whole of the coastal belt of the country, right from Gujarat to Andaman and Nicobar Islands.

Botanically cashewnuts are known as *Anacardium occidentale* Linn. and they belong to Family *Anacardiaceae* Vernacular name is Kaju.

Trees are evergreen with round canopy, 10-12 m tall and 6-7 m in spread. Trunk is strong and may be of 2 m in girth. Bark is brown. Branching is strong but upright.

Leaves are lush green, large, leathery, oval and alternate, fattened with a petiole of almost green colour, round and 0.5 cm long.

Flowers are pinkish white, small and scented usually borne on tips of young branches. Flower stalk swells to form a fleshy sweet mass of edible potion looking like a small apple.

Fruits are kidney shaped, dry with a greyish coloured pericarp, which is hard and irritant. These are white to slightly cream in colour. These are seeds which are oily, bold and 2 x 1 cm in size.

Fruits are used as dry fruits, cashew, apple for brewing and wood for making furniture. It is a good ornamental, shade and avenue tree.

Cashew (apple) fruit contains 86.3 g moisture, protein 0.2 g, fat 0.1 g, mineral matter 0.2 g, fibre 0.9 g, carbohydrates 12.3 g, calcium 10 mg, phosphorus 10 mg, iron 0.2 mg per 100 g while calorific value is 31 Kcal.

Cashew nut, used as nut has 5.9 g moisture, protein 21.2 g, fat 46.9 g, mineral matter 2.4 g, fibre 1.8 g, carbohydrates 22.3 g, calcium 50 mg, phosphorus 450 mg, iron 5.81 mg, carotene 60 g, Thiamine 0.63 mg, Riboflavin 0.19 mg, Niacin 1.2 mg, and calorific value is 596 Kcal per 100 g of nuts.

**Annona Squamosa—
Custard Apple—Sitaphal**

CUSTARD APPLE

It is a fruit tree of the arid region under sub-tropical climate. They can be raised up to 600 m above the mean sea level but are sensitive to frost.

Custard apple belongs to Family *Annonacae* and botanical name is *Annona squamosa* L. In vernacular, it is known as Seetaphal.

Trees are deciduous in nature, small in size, about 4-5 m in height and 3-4 m in spread and assume the shape of a bush. Trunk is smooth and stout. Branching is irregular but the bush has round top.

Leaves are green, alternate, oblong-lanceolate to lanceolate, leathery and of medium size.

Flowers are generally yellow.

Fruits are fleshy syncarp, formed by the fusion of pistils and receptacle, sub-globose, cordate or conical in shape, greenish yellow in colour, 8 cm across, tubercled and pulp is cream, sweet and soft.

Seeds are oblong, brownish black, 0.75 cm in diameter, many, embedded in the soft pulp.

Fruits are eaten fresh and they start rotting very early. The skin assumes blackish colour and pulp becomes acidic or rotton on over-maturity or long storage.

Nutritive value per 100 g of pulp is: moisture 70.5 g, protein 1.6 g, fat 0.4 g, mineral matter 0.9 g, fibre 3.1 g, carbohydrates 23.5 g, calcium 17 mg, phosphorus 47 mg, iron 4.31 mg, magnesium 84 mg, copper 0.45 mg, manganese 0.64 mg, zinc 0.80 mg, chromium 0.026 mg, Thiamine 0.07 mg, Riboflavin 0.17 mg, Niacin 1.3 mg, Vita C 37 mg and calorific value is 104 Kcal.

Fruits are used in puddings and ice-creams. Leaves are used for medicinal purposes due to presence of annonine. Seeds yield oil which is used in soap making and the cake received as a by-product is a cattle feed.

Anthocephalus Cadamba

KADAMBA

Trees are mostly found in sub-tropical areas but are also found near coastal areas in the south of the country. Trees prefer moist to wet tropical climate. They occur in sub-Himalayan tracts of West Bengal, Assam and adjoining areas, and on the West Coast from North Kanara Southwards to Thiruvananthapuram.

Botanical name of the specie is *Anthocephalus cadamba* Miq. and belongs to *Rubiaceae* family, *Anthocephalus indica* is its other name. In vernacular it is known as Kadam.

It is a large graceful tree which is deciduous in nature. Trees may grow as high as 10 m or so with a spread of 5 to 7 m. Trunk may become 2 m in girth when fully matured. Bark is greyish brown. Branching is spreading downward but strong.

Leaves are elliptical, oblong or ovate, shining, glabrous on top and pubescent underneath, lush green, 12-15 cm x 3-5 cm with a strong petiole.

Flowers are of orange colour and glabrous that appear solitary on terminals from June to August, peduncle is green, 2-3 cm long.

Fruits ripen and drop in January-February.

Seeds are minute and many.

Trees are fast growing during the early stage of development.

It is an ornamental tree bearing attractive flowers as balls of golden yellow colour. It is also good shade tree, associated with Lord Krishna and his Rasa Leela. Wood yellowish white and is used for making packing cases, beams and for carving, etc. Leaves are used as fodder. Fruits are eaten by birds and animals.

Arecanut

ARECANUT

Trees are grown in groups as ornamental trees in the coastal areas and sub-tropical region spanning from Gujarat to West Bengal through coastal areas of Karnataka, Kerala, Tamil Nadu, Andhra Pradesh, Orissa, West Bengal including the Andaman and Nicobar Islands.

Supari is the common name in vernacular while botanical name is *Areca catechu* L. and it belongs to Family *Palmae*.

Trees are evergreen in nature found growing on moderate type of soil. Trees are usually tall about 10-15 m in height, slim and palm stemmed. Trunk has scars of fallen leaves.

Leaves are compound, pinnate, glabrous and irregularly toothed with fairly large segments, dark green, usually remain at the top as a bunch or umbrella. Some of the outer leaves are pendulous but are generally erect.

Flowers are unisexual, growing in an inflorescence with branching speadix that appears below the bunch of leaves. Female flowers grow singly at the ramification, surrounded by the smaller, scented male flowers.

Fruit is ovoid, berry, 3-5 cm long, orange coloured, fibre covered nut.

Seed is a nut which has a smooth skin and contains dye stuff.

Fruits are hard but edible when cut into pieces. In fact, they are chewed with betel leaf or other preparations. They are used in worship and for medicinal purposes. Wood also has medicinal properties but is of medium quality.

Fresh arecanut contains 31.3 g moisture, 4.9 g protein, fat 4.4 g, mineral matter 1.0 g, fibre 11.2 g, carbohydrates 47.2 g, calcium 50 mg, phosphorus 130 mg, iron 1.5 mg, carotene 3 mg, magnesium 66 mg, copper 0.92 mg, manganese 1.46 mg, zinc 0.81 mg, chromium 0.473 mg, Vita A 3 I.U., and calorific value is 240 Kcal.

TODDY PALM

They are found growing in tropical to mild-Sub-tropical regions of the country.

Trees are generally known as the Toddy trees. Botanical name is *Arenga pinnata* and it belongs to Family *Palmae.*

Toddy Palm is an evergreen tree, going tall to about 30 m in height with a thick and strong cylindrical trunk and a dense crown.

Leaves are pinnate, 3-5 cm long, compound, green on upper surface while whitish green beneath with black fibre around the leaf axis. They appear nearing top and are drooping, forming umbrella shape canopy.

Flower is long and pendulous, which is either male or female, surrounded by boat shaped bracts. Female flowers are few and scattered.

Fruit is 5-7 cm long, oval or sheprical, turbinate, supported by calyx and corolla and crowned by persistent stigmas.

Seeds are 2-3 in each fruit, compressed or planoconvex, endospermic, white, fleshy and edible.

It is regarded as a sacred tree in the South Indian States and adjoining coastal areas due to its medicinal properties and other domestic uses.

Trees are very attractive when grown in isolation as ornamental or avenue trees. Toddy is a sweet sap extracted from the trees, mostly the male trees. This liquid is used in medicines and for nutritive values. Wood is strong and long lasting (about 100 years). Leaves are used for making paintings and writing.

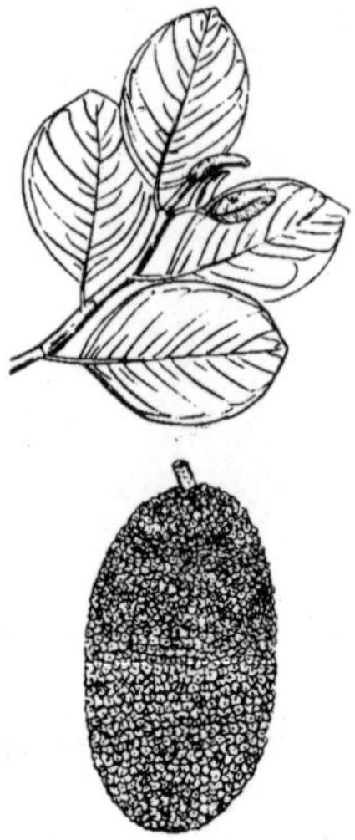

Artocarpus heterophyllus

JACK FRUIT

It is found growing in moist areas in the lower hills, best under the altitudinal range of 600-1000 m above mean sea level. These are also found growing in plains and coastal areas. The tree occurs both in cultivated and wild form.

Jack fruit commonly known as Kathal is botanically *Artocarpus heterophyllus* Lamk. This belongs to the Family *Moraceae*.

The trees are attractive, evergreen, going to height of 15 m or so, with a spread of about 5-6 m when fully developed. Branching is profuse but strong. Bark is brown and exudes milky latex. Crown is dense and round having lush green leaves which are leathery and stiff in structure with a petiole.

Leaves are 10-12 cm long, 5-6 cm in width, elliptical and shining.

Flowers appear at the end of branches or on the trunk and branches away from the leafy area.

Fruits are oval shaped, often 30 cm x 20 cm and even more, green, pimpled and with rough surface. The surface may become yellowish green to brownish green on maturity. They exude latex, which dries up soon on exposure.

Trees are valued for their large sized fruits, which are used when slightly unripe as vegetable or made into pickle. Ripe fruits are juicy and eaten either fresh or their pulp is made into syrup. Seeds are edible. Children like the sweet pulp. The timber is of excellent quality, which is bright yellow when fresh but turns darker on exposure. It is used for quality furniture and for making household articles and handles of tools. Leaves of the trees have medicinal value and are used to cure some skin diseases.

The nutritive value of fruit is well known to the users. Jack-fruit when used for vegetable has 84.0% moisture, 2.6% protein, 0.3% fat, 0.9% carbohydrates to provide 51 Kcal per 100 g. Ripe fruit may contain 76.2% moisture, 1.9% protein, 0.1% fat, 0.9% mineral matter, 1.1% fibre, 19.8% carbohydrates, calcium 0.2%, phosphorus 0.41%, iron 0.05%, Vita A 175 I.U., Thiamine 0.03 mg, Riboflavin 0.13 mg, Niacin 0.4 mg and Vita C 7 mg, and energy released is 88 Kcal per 100 g. Seeds contain 64.5% moisture, 6.6% protein, 0.4% fat, 1.5% fibre, 25.8% carbohydrates and energy is 133 Kcal per 100 g.

Artocarpus Lakoocha

MONKEY JACK

Trees are mostly found in moist tropical regions in sub-Himalayan tract up to 1000 m amsl from Kumaon eastwards to Assam and south to Myanmar and the Andaman and Nicobar Islands, Bihar, Orissa, Madhya Pradesh and in West coast from Konkan southwards to Malabar and Travancore.

It is also known as Lakooch or Dheu in vernacular and its botanical name is *Artocarpus lakoocha* Roxb. and it belongs to Family *Moraceae*.

It is a deciduous tree with a clear straight stem, generally 8-10 m high with a spread of 4-6 m.

Leaves are green.

Flower heads are axillary.

Fruits are earth-coloured, oddly shaped, 8 cm across, juicy, sweet when mature.

Trees are valued for their fruits which are usually pickled when immature but mature fruits are eaten. Raw fruits contain 89.4 g moisture, protein 1.6 g, fat 1.2 g, minerals 1.1 g, fibre 2.8 g, carbohydrates 13.9 g, calcium 67 mg, phosphorus 25 mg, per 100 g while calorofic value is 73 Kcal.

Seeds are used in medicines as purgative. Bark is powdered and used for dusting on soars for healing. Wood is yellowish brown when fresh but turns dark brown after exposure. It is used as industrial timber and as fire wood.

Azadirachta indica

MARGOSA

Trees grow wild in the dry forests to moist tropical forests in the outer Himalayas in valleys particularly the north western parts. They are found growing almost in every State where they can get some moisture in the soil to establish themselves.

Azadirachta indica A. Juss is the botanical name of the tree. Its synonym is *Melia indica* Linn. This belongs to Family *Meliaceae.* Vernacular name is Neem.

Although it is evergreen in nature but may behave deciduous in cooler parts. Trees are moderately tall (8-10 m) with a spread of 4-5 m, canopy is round but kept as umbrella so the bole remains clean up to 3-4 m. Bark is moderately thick of dark grey colour with oblique furrows.

Leaves are compound, green, having 9-13 leaflets crowded near the end of each branch.

Flowers of white yellowish or cream colour, small and many in number appear during the spring.

Fruits become yellow on ripening during summer, which are sweet, pulpy, 2-3 cm long and 1 cm in diameter.

Seeds are hard, round, black or purple in colour. They are also used as beads.

Trees are raised for their leaves, seeds and wood. Leaves are used in a number of ways for medicinal purposes and in keeping away the insects from woollen clothes. Bark is used as tonic and neem oil is extracted from the seeds. The oil is used in many preparations. Oil cake is used as cattle feed and manure. Twigs are used as tooth-brush. Wood is used as timber and fuel. It is a good avenue tree that can be planted along roadsides, paths and other borders.

Neem fruit is eaten, its nutritive value per 100 gm is—moisture 81.9 g, protein 1.3 g, fat 1.0 g, minerals 0.7 g, carbohydrates 15.1 g, calcium 25 mg, phosphorus 41 mg and provide 75 Kcal energy.

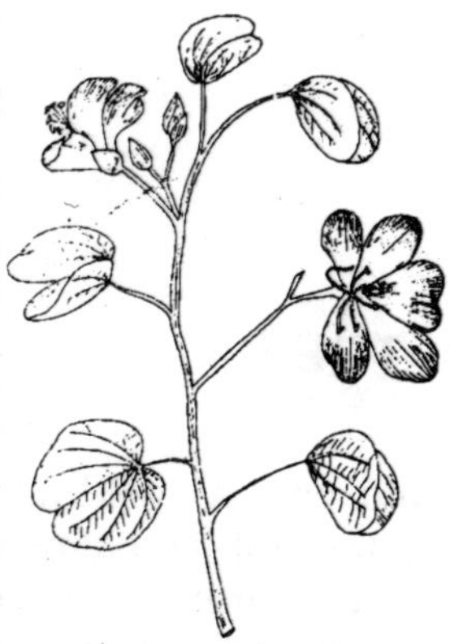

Bauhinia Purpurea Linn

PURPLE BAUHINIA

Trees are found in their natural form in sub-Himalayan tract ascending the outer hills and valleys to 1500 m above mean sea level. It is a tree of moist tropical climate which is found in mixed deciduous forests from Pakistan to Bhutan.

The tree is also known by the name of Khairwal, Karar, Koliar and Kaniar in vernacular at various places. Its botanical name is *Bauhinia purpurea* Linn. belonging to the Family *Caesalpiniaceae,* having the characteristic feature of fixing atmospheric nitrogen through their nodulated roots.

It is an evergreen tree of moderate height with bushy crown and short trunk. Canopy is round. Bark is brown to dark grey and smooth.

Leaves are simple, stalked, blade usually 7-15 cm long, bilobed, veins prominent, radiant from the base, lobes often overlapping along the inner margins.

Flowers are of showy colour, deep pink to purple or deep rose to lilac in colour, appear from September to December, large and fragrant.

Pods are sword like, glabrous, flat, 15-25 cm x 1-2 cm with greenish tinge in the early stage but becomes brown on maturity. These ripen in February-March. Each pod has 10-15 seeds.

It is an ornamental tree usually planted along roadsides or as avenue tree on hill slopes, in valleys, and along water coarses.

Tree has pinkish white wood which turns dark brown on exposure, is used for making agricultural implements and for construction purposes. Bark is used in tanning. Leaves are fed to cattle. Trees also yield gum. Flowers, buds and leaves to some extent are used as pot herbs or for local medicinal use. Wood is also used for timber.

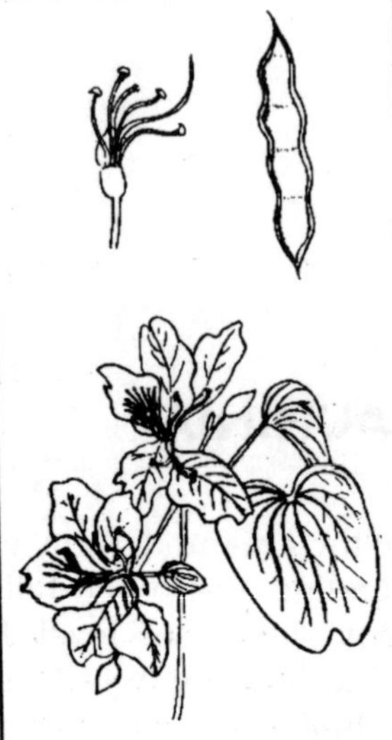

Bauhinia Variegata Kachnar

ORCHID TREE

Trees are mostly found both as wild and in the cultivated form in the sub-Himalayan tract from Indus river eastwards throughout the western Himalaya ascending to 1100 m above mean sea level in moist tropical to sub-tropical climates. The trees are found from Pakistan to Bhutan up to 1800 m altitude.

Trees look beautiful and charming when in full bloom during early spring, just after the emergence of new leaves. The tree known in vernacular as Kachnar belongs to the Family *Caesalpiniaceae*, so have root nodules for fixation of atmospheric nitrogen, through bacteria to enrich the soil fertility. Its botanical name is *Bauhinia variegata* Linn. It is deciduous in nature, i.e. leaves are shed in the autumn season. It is a medium sized tree reaching to the height of 7-8 m with unequal crown. Branching is profuse but irregular.

Leaves are bilobed, round, 11-15 nerved leaflets, thick, green when mature. They are shed in November-December and new leaves appear in March-April.

Flowers appear in February-March, large, white to purple in colour but sometimes colour may be yellowish green or dark purple. These are fragrant.

Pods are 20 cm long, flat, hard, sharp-beaked and narrow having 10-25 seeds. Pods ripen in May-June and dehisce on the tree. The seed is brown, flat, nearly circular and has coriaceous testa.

Leaves are fed to cattle while the buds are used after cooking or boiling as vegetable in various ways. They are also pickled. Tree yields timber. Bark is astringent and used as a tonic and for cure of various skin disorders and ulcers. Dried buds are used to cure piles and dysentery. Bark is sometimes used for tanning and dyeing of fibre. Wood is grey and moderately hard and is used for construction of building and other purposes.

Betula Alnoides

KATH

Trees are found in temperate and sub-tropical forests, near ravines, stream sides in the Himalayas from the Sutlej River eastward between 1500-3000 m above mean sea level from Himachal Pradesh to South West China. Trees are also seen in Khasi Hills and Manipur.

Botanical name of the tree is *Betula alnoides* Buch. and the Family name is *Betulaceae*. Trees are deciduous in nature. It is a moderate to large sized tree that may grow as tall as 30 m or so. Bark is papery, greyish brown to reddish in colour, which peels off in thick rolls.

Leaves are ovate to ovate-lanceolate, acute, 8-15 cm long, very irregularly doubly saw-toothed and are hairy beneath when young and gland rotted when mature.

Long slender female catkins appear during winter, which are usually clustered in 2-4.

Fruit is a nut.

Nutlets have a wing broader than itself, bracts with 2 small lobes or teeth.

Leaves are lopped for fodder especially for goat. Heartwood is brownish but sapwood is white. Wood is moderately hard and heavy. It is easy to work so used for cabinet work, tool handles, planks, etc.

Betula Utilis

BIRCH

Trees are known for their bark, which is papery and peels off horizontally and is believed to be used as a paper for writing during ancient times.

Birch in vernacular is known as the Bhojpatra.

Bhojpatra trees are seen in forests right from Pakistan to Southwest China including Sikkim and Bhutan. In inner Himalayas, they are found growing in Jammu-Kashmir, Himachal Pradesh and hills of Uttaranchal between 2700-4300 m elevation. They are best under the open spaces.

Trees are known by the name of birch, which is of many kinds. In India we get *Betula utilis* D. Don. belonging to Family *Betulaceae.* Trees are deciduous in nature.

It is a moderate sized tree. Bark is white to brownish black which peels off in very thin, pale and almost transparent horizontal strips, inner layer is of pink colour.

Leaves are woolly haired beneath, 5-8 cm, ovate, fine pointed, irregularly saw toothed, hairy when young.

Male catkins are 5-10 cm long, reddish, appear on bare branches along with new leaves. Female spikes are solitary, 2.5-4 cm x 1-2 cm, appear during early spring.

Nutlets are 2 mm across, winged with a 3 lobed much longer bract.

Wood is used for building purposes. Bark is used as paper for waterproofing and roofing houses.

Bombax malabaricum

COTTON TREE

This tree is found growing throughout the country both in tropical and sub-tropical regions, which ascend up to 1200 m or so in the hilly areas of Western Himalayas in sub-tropical and moist tropical climate, right from Kashmir to Bhutan, spanning in Himachal Pradesh and Uttaranchal.

It is a lofty tree of deciduous nature belonging to the Family *Bombaceae* and its botanical name is *Bombax ceiba* Linn. Syn. *B. malabaricum* D.C. In vernacular, they are known by the name of Semal or Semul and Kapok. The trees are generally 10-15 m tall with spreading but strong branches, which are mostly whorled. Bark is pale pink to brown in colour, smooth in early years but rough on maturity with irregular cracks. Trunk is buttressed at the base.

Foliage is though sparse but enough to provide good canopy. Leaves are green, leathery/glabrous, palmate, compound, 5-7 leaflets, lanceolate, 10-25 cm long and petioled.

Flowers of bright crimson or reddish yellow colour appear in large clusters in the axil of fallen leaves and appear before the emergence of new leaves during early spring. The flowers do last for a month.

Pods are long, woody, dark brown, 10-12 cm long and splitting by 5 valves from the top to bottom to release small black seeds enveloped in fine silky wool which provides the tree the name of Cotton Tree.

Trees are multipurpose in their use. They are planted as avenue trees, showy, ornamental, roadside plantation and on boundary forming a fence. It is a good soil-binding tree, which is resistant to drought bur fairly resistant to frost. The floss from the seeds is the silk cotton of commerce and is used for stuffing pillows and cushions and as insulating material. Gum from the bark has a medicinal value while the leaves are a source of medium quality fodder.

Butea monosperma

FLAME OF THE FOREST

It is called Flame of the Forest, since the flowers borne on the trees during the early spring before the emergence of leaves are of deep red to crimson colour and they look like a flame, which provides a graceful appearance to these trees.

Butea monosperma Lamk is botanical name and is known as Dhak or Palash in vernacular.

Trees belong to Family *Papilionaceae* and is found in the sub-Himalayan tract and plains of the country, chiefly in the mixed or dry forests of central and western India but is also more common in the plains and upper region of the hills in the western Himalayas. Trees are found in all types of locations and conditions of growth and hence are useful for reclamation of poor, saline or wastelands.

It is a deciduous, medium-sized tree going almost 10 m high with a strong trunk and crooked or irregular branches. Bark is fibrous and of light brown to grey colour.

Leaves are compound of 3 leaflets, large, green, shining on the upper surface while tomentose on the lower side.

Flowers appear during summer in small clusters on leafless branches, bright deep red tinged and hanging.

Pods are oblong, hairy, 15 cm x 3 cm, cylindrical, black or shining dark brown, and contain a single seed.

Seeds are flat, 3-4 cm long and 2.5 cm broad amd 1 mm thick.

Trees are highly valued as host trees for lac-culture. Flowers yield yellow colour; bark and seeds have medicinal properties. Gum is also extracted. Leaves are used for making various kinds of plates for serving food. Wood can withstand moisture so is used for making various agricultural implements and tools.

Callistemon Viminalis

BOTTLE BRUSH TREE

They are found in the mid-hills to lower areas and valleys between the altitudinal range of 400 m to 2000 m above mean sea level.

Generally these trees are raised as small trees but they may grow as tall trees going as high as 10-15 m in exceptional cases where they get good soil and ambient climate. They also grow best in plains and warmer areas.

It belongs to the Family *Myrtaceae.* There are two species in common use, *Callistemon lanceolatus* D.C. Sweet and *Callistemon viminalis* Gerten. G. Don. f. Both are evergreen in nature. Main trunk is strong but only upto 3 m and then due to pendulous branching it becomes weak.

Leaves are lanceolate, small, green, borne in clusters, narrow and chanelled.

Bottle brush shaped flowers appear in terminal clusters in March and October, their colour is usually scarlet but may be purplish or yellowish. These flowers provide a graceful look to the trees.

Pods are capsular. Seeds are many and minute.

These trees are ornamental in nature and are planted along roadsides, borders or in centre of a lawn as an ornamental tree.

Trees are largely planted as an ornamental tree in gardens. It is also suitable for planting singly in lawns or in small clumps.

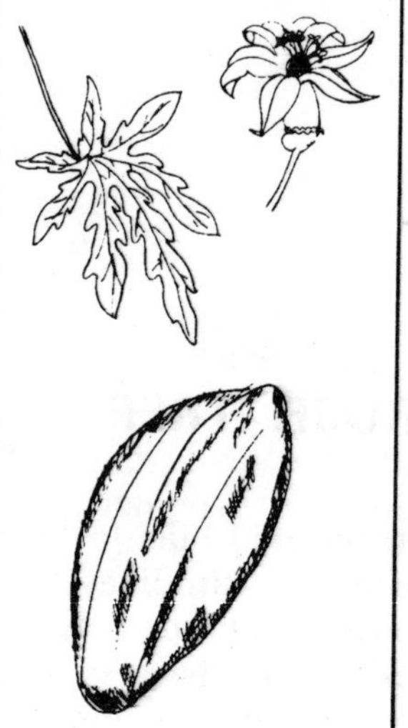

Carica Papaya

PAPAYA

It is also known as Papita, which is found common in the lower hills, and valley areas, in pockets where spring frost is of few occurrences. In fact, it is a sub-tropical fruit tree, which has found place in the hills of Western and Eastern Himalayas. It is an important crop of the tropical and sub-tropical region where it is grown as a cash crop on large scale.

Papaya in hills is raised as a petty fruit tree as it is highly susceptible to cool conditions. Both trees and fruits are not able to tolerate chilly winds. Fruits are also attacked by birds.

Papaya (*Carica papaya* Linn.) belonging to Family *Caricaceae,* is an evergreen small tree (3-5 m), which is usually single stemmed having umbrella like canopy of long petioled leaves of green colour, which fall off and on so give place for the new leaves to emerge. Leaves are compound.

Flowers are pale green while fruit is a berry of green to yellow colour, soft skinned but smooth, oval to round in shape, may be conical at the free end. Size 10-20 cm x 20-25 cm and may weight from 1.5 kg to 3 kg. Pulp is yellowish orange, sweet scented lined with the upper skin, 2-5 cm thick and free end is lined with brown to black seeds of round shape. They may be few to many in a single fruit.

The nutritive value of papaya fruit as indicated per 100 g is as follow—moisture 90.8 g, protein 0.6 g, fat 0.1 g, mineral matter 0.5 g, fibre 0.8 g, carbohydrates 7.2 g, calcium 17 mg, phosphorus 13 mg, iron 0.5 mg, magnesium 11 mg, potassium 69 mg, sulphur 13 mg, Vita A 2020 I.U., Thiamine 40 mg, Niacin 0.2 mg, Riboflavin 250 mg, ascorbic acid 46 mg. Calorific value is 38 Kcal.

Since it is a semi-woody tree, the wood is of less value and is only used as fuel. Papain is extracted from unripe fruits while ripe fruits are used for dessert purposes. At some places green papaya is cooked as a vegetable.

Carpinus Viminea

LOLTI

Trees are found growing in forests under shady places, near rivers, water coarses, etc. in the Himalayas east of the Chenab River to Southwest China through Himachal Pradesh, Uttaranchal, West Bengal, etc., at elevations between 1500-2700 m.

It is also known by the name of Shinrai, Shangri, Phamnai, etc. in vernacular and its botanical name is *Carpinus viminea* Lindley/Wall. It belongs to Family *Betulaceae/Corylaceae.*

Trees are deciduous in nature. Tree size is medium with compact grey bark that has darker streaks. Branches are slender and drooping.

Leaves are glabrous, ovate-lanceolate, long petioled, doubly saw toothed, 5-12 cm long. Stipules oblong, which soon fall off.

Male catkins are pendulous, 8 cm long and borne on leafless branches. Female flowers are borne in pendulous clusters, which are 5-10 cm long.

Nuts are 3 mm across, ribbed with lanceolate toothed involucres, 7.5 cm with small triangular basal lobes.

Wood is used as fuel. Leaves are lopped as fodder for goat and it is of medium quality.

Carya Illinoiensis

PECAN NUT

It is a cultivated tree introduced for its fruits, known as nuts and are used as dry fruits. Trees have been planted in the region where they get sufficient chill of about 400 hours around 7°C during winter and followed by a growing period of about 8 months in which the temperature remains around 25°C. Trees are tolerant to drought conditions for some period but continuous drought or dry spell causes drying of leaves.

Pecan-nut is *Carya illinoiensis* L. belonging to the Family *Juglandaceae*. Trees are deciduous with upright branching, height may be 20 m or so with a spread of 6-10 m and trunk diameter may be up to 2 m. Canopy is mostly ovoid round. Bark is of light-brown colour.

Leaves are compound with 9 to 17 lanceolate short-stalked leaflets, green on upper side but pale yellow from below.

Fruit is ellipsoidal in shape, borne in cluster of 3-10, 4 cm x 2 cm with dark brown hard husk, inside the hard husk is the nut having a thin shell of light to dark brown skin containing two large kernels which are usually of cream colour.

Various parts of the tree are of use to mankind. Nuts are eaten as such when matured or after roasting and salting. The powder of hard shell of the fruit can be used for filling the abrasive surface before painting. Wood is used for furniture making and other uses since it does not shrivel when wet.

Nutritive value per 100 g of kernels is: moisture 3.4 g, fat 72.2 g, protein 9.2 g, carbohydrates 14.6 g, fibre 2.3 g, calcium 73 mg, phosphorus 289 mg, magnesium 24 mg, iron 2.4 mg, Vita A 130 I.U., Thiamine 0.86 mg, Riboflavin 0.13 mg, Niacin 0.90 mg, ascorbic acid 2 mg, Calorific value is 687 Kcal. Oleic acid in the seed may be from 51 to 77 per cent depending upon the variety.

Cassia Fistula

INDIAN LABURNUM TREE

Though the tree of the species *Cassia* commonly known as Amaltas in vernacular are found almost throughout the country in the tropical and sub-tropical climates but is more common in moist tropical deciduous forests, shrubberies and open spaces/places in the Himalayas stretching from India to Myanmar up to an altitude of 1500 m or so in the mid-hills and valleys of the outer Himalayas and Shivalik ranges.

Cassia fistula Linn. belongs to Family *Caesalpiniaceae* which can fix the atmospheric nitrogen though its nodules into the soil to increase the fertility. It is a moderate sized tree of deciduous nature going up to 10 m or so. Branches are strong and slightly bent upward. Bark is greenish grey or light dark brown in colour.

Leaves are compound, in 3-8 pairs, pinnate, leaflets 5-15 cm long, leathery, copper coloured when young or tender but turns green on maturity.

Flowers are large about 5 cm across which appear in long pendulous bunches of large, bright yellow colour during April-June.

Pods are fairly long, 30-50 cm x 2 cm, cylindrical like a pipe.

Seeds are contained in sweet pulp, which is brown. There are many seeds in a pod and seeds are flat and brown to glossy black.

The tree is an ornamental tree as the flowers are attractive. Wood of the tree being highly durable is used for making handles of implements. Bark is used for tanning and medicinal purposes. The tree is drought resistant but not tolerant to frost and is good for wasteland development in valley areas.

Castanea Sativa

SPANISH CHEST NUT

This specie is different from the Horse Chest nut but resambles in shape of fruit only. It is a nut tree of temperate climate found growing in the sub-tropical regions where sufficiently low temperature during winter is available. These trees are mostly found in high hills of the temperate region but not in high alpine region and so limited upto the altitude of 3000 m.

Chestnut belongs to Family *Fagaceae* and its botanical name is *Castanea sativa* Mill.

Trees are deciduous in nature, shedding their leaves during autumn. Height of the tree may be 20 m or so and is a long-lived tree of more than 1000 years. Canopy is round but wide. Bark of mature tree is ridged and of grey brown colour. Branching is profuse and branches are stout and spreading.

Leaves are large, oblong-lanceolate, main and secondary veins are distinctly raised.

Flowers are unisexual, male flowers grow in erect catkins while the females, numbering 1-3 are joined in a distinctive cupule.

Wood is used for manufacture of furniture and building house. Fruits are edible. Young trees have rapid growth and coppice readily.

Casuarina equisetifolia

CASUARINA

Though the specie is mostly found in the tropics but in the Himalayas, these are found growing in valleys and moist areas upto 1500 m above mean sea level. They relish the temperate climate, particularly the cooler nights and the annual rainfall range of 700-2000 mm. Thus, they are found growing in lower to mid-hills in sub-tropical region of this country.

Trees are evergreen in nature and botanical name is *Casuarina equisetifolia* Forst. which belongs to the Family *Casuarinaceae.*

Height of tree may go upto 30 m but generally they are kept 10-20 m tall with a spread of 5-6 m. Branches are green, slender and look like thick pine needles and drooping. Bark is brown, rough, fibrous which peels-off in longitudinal strips. Internodes are wire like, often 0.5 cm long.

Leaves are whorled, reduced to minute scales or teeth, broadly oblong.

Flowers are unisexual which appear twice a year; February to April and September-October. Male spikes about 0.5 cm long while female spikes are small and in dense heads.

Fruit is woody cone. short stalked, globose, 1 cm in diameter. Fruits ripen in June and December.

Seeds are greyish, 1 seeded samara, 1 cm in diameter.

Trees are used as wind-breaks, ornamental, for pole and for fuel, charcoal and soil conservation. Pulp is also used. Wood is very hard and liable to crack and split. Excellent for fuel. It is grown in plantations and used in afforestation works.

Cedrus Deodara

HIMALAYAN CEDAR

Trees are of majestic shape for which they are raised in forests in the temperate region in the altitudinal range of 1200 m to 4000 m above mean sea level. The trees are found in all the States falling under the lap of Indian Himalayas right from Afghanistan to Arunachal Pradesh. They are found in forests in mid-hills in all these States on various types of soils.

Deodar is also known as Kelon, Kelu and Diar and is regarded as a sacred (the tree of gods) tree since its wood is of prime importance.

It is an evergreen tree belonging to genus *Cedrus* of the Family *Coniferaeae* and the botanical name is *Cedrus deodara* Linn.

The trees are long-lived about 700 years or so when kept under good management. The crown of young trees is conical which becomes round as the tree grows old. Bark is smooth, dark brown, fissures vertical. Branching is almost flat but the branches are spreading. Leaves are sharp pointed and needle like which are usually dark green in colour, smooth and shining.

Flowers appear as male and female cones on the same tree. Generally, male flowers appear in June and shed yellow pollens as dust during September-October. Female cones appear in August which are smaller than male cones but after pollination and fertilization grow into large size (8-10 cm x 5-7 cm) and attain the chocolate brown colour on maturity and release the winged triangular rounded seeds in October of the next year.

It is a good avenue tree when raised in the mid of a lawn or along the roadside. It is used for construction of temples, royal palaces, common places and houses. Much of the wood is used for making railway sleepers. It provides a clean and good finish to the surface. Cedar oil is used in perfumery and soap industry. Wood, sawdust and oil has medicinal value. Cones are used as fuel and young branches are used for decoration.

Deodar trees provide shelter to a number of other plant species like *Viola canescens*, Ivy, *Rubus* spp, wild rose, etc. These are sensitive to drought but hardy to frost and can tolerate heavy snow-fall.

Celtis Australis

KHIRAK

Trees are best under temperate Himalaya in altitudinal range of 1300-2700 m above mean sea level. It grows from about 500-2500 m elevation in North-Western Himalayas in Jammu and Kashmir, Himachal Pradesh and Uttaranchal and in other States North-Eastern Himalayas, mostly on well drained clayey loam soil.

Khirak is known by the botanical name *Celtis australis* Linn. and this belongs to the Family *Utricaceae.*

Trees are evergreen, which shed leaves on the onset of winter season, and new leaves appear in spring. Canopy is round and main trunk is strong and straight. Height of the tree may be 25 m or so with a thick trunk and rounded crown. Bark is grey and smooth. Young branched are downy.

Leaves alternate, short-stalked, nearly glabrous, ovate, 7-12 cm, long pointed, sharply toothed, base very unequal, downy underneath.

Blooms in April-May. Flowers are pale yellow in colour appearing before or along the leaves, polygamous, male in clusters or short racemes; female flowers appear in axils of upper leaves.

Fruit is a long stalked, ovoid, usually solitary, drupe, 1 cm long, more or less woolly at the base.

Seed is hard and wrinkled.

It is a good foliage tree, which is regarded as an ornamental tree and is planted near villages and other places, apart in the forests. Wood is light and used for making handles of whips and for inlaid work. Leaves are lopped for fodder.

Cinnamomum Tamala

INDIAN CASSIA

Trees are found in tropical and sub-tropical Himalayas between the elevations of 1000 m to 2700 m. They are seen from Kashmir to Bhutan from 450 m to 2100 m above mean sea level.

Botanical name of the plant is *Cinnamomum tamala* Nees and Eberm. belonging to the Family *Lauraceae.* In vernacular, the tree is known as Tejpatra tree or simply Tejpat.

It is an aromatic tree, which is evergreen in nature and grows to the height of 8-10 m and may attain a girth of 1-5 m or so. Bark is thin and extremely aromatic.

Leaves are bright pink when young and later turns green, long petioled, leathery, glabrous, opposite or nearly so, often alternate, aromatic when crushed.

Flowers are minute, in large hairy clusters, pale yellowish in terminal and axillary branched clusters.

Fruits are succulent and black when ripe, ovoid, 12 mm across.

Trees are of religious importance for Hindu community.

Trees are valued for their leaves and oil. Leaves are used as spice and medicine as a carminative and in colic disorder and diarrhoea. Leaves both fresh and dried are used in Indian cookery while fresh leaves are substituted for betel leaves. Thin brown bark is used as a substitute for the common cinnamon in cookery and other food preparations. Oil is extracted from the bark, which is pale yellow in colour and is used in perfumery and pharmaceutical preparations.

Citrus Limon

LEMON

They are found growing almost in all the areas falling under the Himalayas right from the foothills to 4000 m above mean sea level. Scattered plantations are seen in the valleys of all the hilly States of the Himalayan belt. They are also raised at lower elevations, right from the sea-coast to the lower hills.

Botanical name of the tree is *Citrus limon* Burm. F. and it belongs to Family *Rutaceae.* It is an evergreen small tree, which is almost bushy in nature.

Tree height is 4-6 m with an equal spread and a round crown. Main trunk is usually branched forming haphazard branches. There are thorns on branches.

Leaves are 5-7 cm x 1.5-2 cm, elliptical-acuminate with crenate margins, lush green on upper side while light green on the lower side, ribs are prominent, petiole is light to greyish green, round and 1 to 2 cm long.

Flowers are scented, white, small and almost not visible from a distance.

Fruits may be oval to round or oblong, pale yellow to greenish yellow, thin skinned, almost 0.2 cm thick, shining and oily; 3 cm across, juicy, sour flesh containing the ovoid seeds, 1-2 seeds in each loculii.

Seeds are creamish white; round on one side while pointed on the other side, 0.25-0.35 cm x 0.2-0.25 cm.

Nutritive value per 100 g is—moisture 85.0 g, protein 1.0 g, fat 0.9 g, carbohydrates 11.1 g, fibre 1.7 g, mineral matter 0.3 g, calcium 0.07 g, phosphorus 0.01 g, iron 0.3 g, Vita A in traces, Thiamine 0.2 mg, Niacin 0.1 mg, Riboflavin 0.4 mg and Vita C 39 mg. Calorific value is 57 Kcal.

These are bushy trees that provide slightly acidic fruit, which are used in a number of ways. The trees may be used as a fence or a wind-break.

Juice of the fruit is used for making squash and other products. Fruits are cut into pieces and used in salad. They are pickled in many ways. Vita C content is rich in these fruits and so provide refreshing drink. Oil from the skin is used in a number of perfumery and pharmaceutical preparations. Wood is used as fuel.

Citrus nobilis

MANDARIN

These are sub-tropical fruit trees that are commercially raised in orchards mostly in the sub-tropical regions of the country. They are almost found in all the States but best production in the valleys and lower hills where nights are bit pleasant at the time of maturity of the fruits. They are found up to 500 m above mean sea level. Lower belts of Himachal Pradesh, Uttaranchal, Jammu, North Eastern states, Madhya Pradesh, Gujarat, and many other States have systematic orchards.

Botanical name is *Citrus nobilis* and the syn. is *Citrus reticulata* while the Family name is *Rutaceae*. Vernacular name is Sangtra.

Trees are evergreen in nature and are medium sized often going up to 5 m with a spread of about 5 m. Canopy may be round or oval but is spreading. Bark is light brown, scaly and cracking in older trees but is green in the earlier stages.

Leaves are lush green, leathery, glossy on upper surface but slightly light green and rough on the lower side, 7-8 cm x 3-5 cm with pointed tips and green stalks that may be 1 cm long.

Flowers are small, white and scented, often hiding under the foliage and they appear during late spring or summer.

Fruits are flattened spheroids of a bright orange colour, berries and have a thin peel that comes off easily. Flesh is sweet and juicy with a pleasant smell. Size may be 6-7 cm x 5-6 cm.

Seeds are many, cream coloured and pointed on both sides but slightly flattened on sides and swollen in the mid.

Trees are mainly grown for their fruits that are rich source of ascorbic acid. The nutritive value is : 100 g of pulp contains 87.8 g moisture, 0.3 g fat, 0.9 g protein, 10.6 g carbohydrates, 0.4 g minerals, 0.05 g calcium, 0.02 g phosphorus, 0.1 g iron, 350 I.U. Vita A, 0.12 mg Thiamine, 0.3 mg Riboflavin, 0.6 mg Niacin, Vita C 68 mg and calorific value is 49 Kcal.

Peel of the fruit is used for extraction of essential oil used for flavouring and in perfumery medicines. Wood is not of good quality hence used for fuel and firewood.

Citrus Sinensis

SWEET ORANGE

It is believed that the species originated in China and is grown in many countries. The trees are found both in the tropical and sub-tropical regions where they get milder nights during the maturity of fruits. Like other citrus fruits, they are raised in commercial plantations in almost every State. These trees can be grown successfully in the hills up to an altitude of 1500 m above mean sea level where there is no frost.

Citrus sinensis is the botanical name and family is *Rutaceae* while the local name may be Narangi, Mosambi or Malta.

Trees are evergreen in nature and they are usually 5 x 5 m with a round to oval canopy. Bark is scaly; trunk is usually small and may have spines. Branching may be horizontal with spines.

Leaves are lush green on upper side while less green with prominent veins on the lower side, 4 to 10 cm long and 1 to 2 cm wide with narrow tip and rounded base having a stalk of 1 cm. Petioles are usually winged.

Flowers are of white colour, fragrant and appear singly in clusters. They bloom in spring i.e., February-March.

The fruit is a berry, 6 - 8 cm across, yellow to orange or green and yellow when ripe, the pulp may be yellowish white or reddish white.

There are many seeds placed in the juice sacs, light cream or white, almost swollen in the middle and round on one side and tapering on the end uniting with the sac.

Trees are mostly found growing in systematic orchards for commercial purpose of selling fruits. They are good for dessert and juice extraction. Essential oil extracted from the peel is used in perfumery and for flavouring foods. Wood is not of good quality.

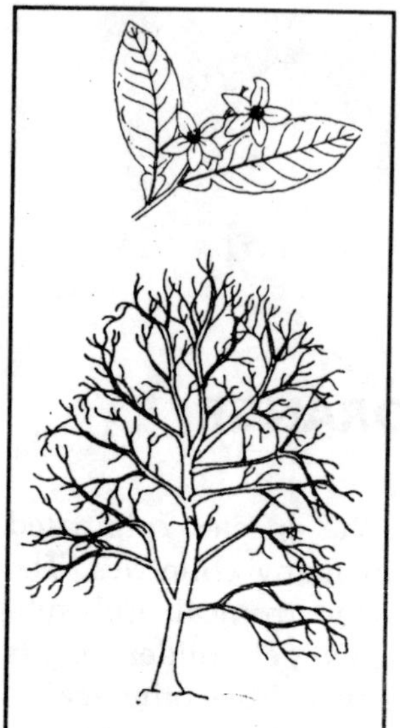

Citrus Pseudo-Limon

HILL LEMON

It is a tree of the cool climate in the sub-tropical region, which extends in the valleys or foothills of the sub-Himalayan tract. Scattered trees are seen here and there on mountain slopes in the mid-hill to low-hill zones of Jammu-Kashmir, Himachal Pradesh and Uttaranchal. Trees can tolerate fair amount of cold but during the initial stage of their establishment, they may be killed by frost or snowfall.

Botanical name of the tree is *Citrus pseudo-limon* var. decumana and the tree belongs to the Family *Rutaceae.* Vernacular name is Galgal.

Trees are evergreen but they do shed their leaves on the arrival of new flush of growth, Dioecious in nature. Trees are deep rooted with a good spread of both roots and upper portions. Trees may be as tall as 10-15 m with a spread of about 6-8 m when full mature. Main trunk is almost straight and bearing branches at regular to irregular distance. There may be some thorns over it. The branches are stout and upright.

Leaves are green, dark on the upper side while light green on the lower side, veins are prominent, petiole is 2-3 cm long, round and green, leaf size is 8-15 cm x 3-5 cm, leathery and shining.

Flowers are plenty, fragrant, small, single in the axis of leaves, in corymbose racemes.

Fruits are quite large, round to oval, some may have projection or protuberance towards the free end, 10-15 cm x 5-7 cm, greenish yellow to pale yellow in colour, shining when young but dull on maturity, upper skin is 0.5 cm thick and is sour; juicy, many seeded.

Seeds are yellowish to creamy white, placed in juice very close to central axis.

Trees are good soil binders and the wood is used for fuel and as fire wood. Fruits are used for extracting juice and then this juice is used in a number of ways. It provides a refreshing drink. Fruits are pickled. Peel of the fruit is used for making marmalade. Essential oil is extracted from the rind.

Cocos Nucifera

COCONUT

Trees in abundance are found growing in tropical and coastal areas of warm wet climate, most predominant States which produce coconuts are the Kerela, Tamil Nadu, Karnataka, Orissa, Andhra Pradesh, West Bengal and the Andaman and Nicobar Islands. They are also found scattered in the adjoining areas.

Vernacular name is Nariyal. Its botanical name is *Cocos nucifera* and the Family is *Palmae.*

Trees are evergreen but do shed their leaves off and on and leave the scar on the trunk. Trees may attain the height of over 20 m having umbrella shaped canopy on top of the main trunk. Stem is cylindrical and tapers towards top. Bark is dark brown to blackish brown.

Leaves are green, compound, pointed with slender leaflets along the main axis like a feather.

Flowers are yellowish in colour, small in size and appear in thick bunches on numerous spikes. Each bunch is covered by a spathe.

Fruits are borne in clusters below the leaf canopy. 30 cm x 25 cm in size with an impermeable cover of green colour which turns brown on ripening. Below is a fibrous layer of 4-5 cm thickness which is around a round or oval nut having a thick shell of 0.25 cm thickness of brown colour, below which is again a thin layer of brown colour encircling the endospermic layer followed by coconut milk. This milk dries up to form a layer of 1 cm thickness.

Fruits are valued for the medicinal and nutritive values which are quite known to the users. Nuts are used for worshipping, fibre for filling cushions and mattresses while hard nut is used for decoration. Trees are both of ornamental value and as an avenue tree. Coconut oil is used for various purposes like cooking and in cosmetics.

The nutritive value of fresh coconut is 36.3 g moisture, 4.5 g, protein, 41.6 g fat, 1.0 g mineral matter, 3.6 g fibre, 13.0 g carbohydrates, 10 mg calcium, 240 mg phosphorus, 1.7 mg iron, 0.05 mg Thiamine, 0.10 mg Riboflavin, 0.8 mg Niacin, 12.5 mg Folic acid, 1 mg Vita C and calorific value is 444 Kcal per 100 g.

Cordia myxa

LASORA

Trees are mostly found growing in drier parts of the sub-tropical and tropical areas in almost whole of the country except the hills since it can tolerate drought but can not withstand frost. It is mostly cultivated along the roads or gardens.

It is known by various names in vernacular like Lehsua, Gonds, etc., but its botanical name is *Cordia myxa* Roxb. and it belongs to family *Boraginaceae*.

Trees are evergreen in nature and are small in size, often ranging between 3-5 m with a spread of 3-4 m, mostly like a big bush. Trunk is strong with upright branches which are mostly crooked. Bark is brown in colour.

Leaves are green, large, 3-5 nerved at the base, simple, alternate and flat, nerved at the base.

Flowers are white in colour which are borne axillary in bunches.

Fruit is a drupe of green colour which turns yellowish green on ripening and even turns pink to brown or black on maturity. Smooth, round to oval, 1 cm x 2 cm and has remains of calyx at the united end. Pulp is green, mucilagenous and viscous but sweet round the seed. Thickness of pulp may be 0.5 to 0.75 cm.

Seeds are small, one in each fruit, hard, pinkish brown.

Fruits are used for the pickling. They contain about 70% mucilagenous pulp which is rich in sugar. Bushes are good as windbreaks, hedge plants and best suited for arid wasteland development.

Cryptomeria Japonica

JAPANESE CEDAR

Sometimes, the trees are referred as Japanese Red Cedar. Trees require high humidity for their best growth and hence are found in humid areas in the sub-tropical region in the Himalayan belt spanning from Pakistan to Bhutan. Trees are found isolated in such climate since they have not been planted on commercial scale as they are sensitive to frost and lightning. They are seen from 1300 m to 2600 m above mean sea level, extensively in Darjeeling area.

Cryptomeria japonica is the botanical name and the Family is *Taxodiaceae.*

Trees are evergreen in nature often going as tall as 30 m with a straight trunk. Crown is pyramidal. Bark is reddish brown, fibrous, which peels off in long strips. Foliage is dense green.

Leaves are arranged spirally and remain for 5 years, 1-2 cm long, flat and have roughly rectangular shape, bright green in summer and dirty red-bronze in winter.

Flowers are monoecious, male catkins are 0.5 to 2 cm long and clustered. Female cones are brown, globose, 1.5-2.0 cm, composed of 20-30 overlapping cone scales.

Matured cones are spherical, terminal and ripen in the first year but remain on the tree even after dissemination of seeds.

Seeds are 0.5 cm, angular, compressed with a sharp narrow edge.

Trees are very good for ornamental, shade, avenue and landscaping purposes. Wood is excellent for furniture and building construction. Cones are used as fuel.

Cydonia Vulgaris

QUINCE

It is a cultivated tree of North-West Himalayan region and is found growing scattered on light soils in the lower to mid-hills.

Botanical name is *Cydonia vulgaris* and it belongs to family *Rosaceae*.

Trees are deciduous in nature, which shed their leaves during autumn or early winter, and new leaves appear in early March or so.

It is small sized tree going to the height of 4 to 5 m with a spread of 5 m or so. Trunk bears many shoots and as such the trunk remains short. Leaves are alternate, short stalked, oval and entire, 8-10 cm long, green on upper surface and downy grey on dorsal side.

Flowers are solitary, small, petals are white from inside and pink or pale red from outside which provide whitish look to the bloom.

Fruit is a pome; pear shaped but sometimes apple shaped. Hollow on both ends and sometimes pointed towards the stalk, golden yellow, scented with hard flesh, slightly astringent.

They contain 8.5-7 g moisture, 0.3 g protein, 0.1 g fat, 0.3 g mineral matter, 1.7 g fibre, 11.9 g carbohydrates, 10 mg calcium, 20 mg phosphorus, 0.4 mg iron, Thiamine 0.02 mg, Riboflavin 0.02 mg, Niacin 0.02 mg, Vita C 11 mg and energy released is 50 Kcal.

Fruits are edible when processed and preserved in sugar.

Twigs are used for raising seedlings. Wood is used for domestic uses.

Dalbergia latifolia

ROSEWOOD

Trees are mostly found growing in the sub-Himalayan tract and valley areas and even in the central and southern parts of the country where they are found scattered in mixed deciduous forests. In the Western Ghats and in the fairly moiost deciduous forests of Southern India, trees attain larger dimensions.

Botanical name of the species is *Dalbergia latifolia* Roxb. It belongs to family *Papilionaceae*. Vernacular name is Shisham or Sitsal.

Trees are usually deciduous but may behave as evergreen. They are large sized with full rounded canopy but trees usually go straight. Bark is thin, grey and ex-foliating in longitudinal flakes.

Leaflets 3-7, broadly elliptic, orbicular or elliptic-obovate, obtuse, sometimes emarginate and 1-6 cm long. Leafless during February-March.

Flowers are whitish, 0.5 cm long on pedicels nearly as long as calyx tube, in short axillary much branched panicles. Blooms from monsoon to autumn.

Fruit is a pod that is oblong lanceolate, 1-4 seeded. They ripen during December to March.

Trees are valued for their fine and durable wood for carving, wood-work and for ornamental purposes. Heartwood is dark purple with black streaks.

Dalbergia Sissoo

SHISHAM

A common tree of tropical and sub-tropical regions is grown extensively in valleys and lower hills of the Himalaya, particularly the sub-Himalayan tract and in the Himalayan valleys up to an elevation of 1500 m. It is seen along streams almost everywhere and on freshly exposed soils along roads, paths, landslides, etc. Being a hardy tree can tolerate even minus 4°C temperature but moist climate is must for best growth.

Though it is a deciduous tree but may behave as evergreen under some conditions. Botanical name of the tree is *Dalbergia sissoo* Roxb. and this belongs to Family *Papillonaceae*. Vernacular name is Shisham or Tahli.

Trees are moderately tall going up to 25 m or so. Spread is also 6-10 m. Trunk is usually straight. Branches are strong but pendulous. Bark is light brown and scaly. Canopy is oval or umbrella shaped.

Leaves are light green when young which become lush green on maturity, odd-pinnate, leaflets 3 or 5, alternate, broadly ovate; 7 x 5 cm with a long tip. They fall during autumn and new leaves emerge out in January or February.

Flowers sessile, yellowish white, 0.75 cm long, axillary panicles, which appear almost along with the leaves during spring.

Pods are green when young and they attain full size by July and start ripening and changing their colour to brown, which is of ripe pods. They ripe during November-December. Pods are like straps with 1-3 seeds, glabrous, 5-8 cm long and papery.

Seeds are brown, round, flat and small.

Trees are mostly planted along roadside for shade. They are good avenue trees except that they shed their leaves, which may hamper the beauty of lawn. Wood is of excellent quality, hard, durable, strong and smooth so used for furniture making, etc. Leaves are fed to cattle, particularly, when they are succulent. Good for silo making.

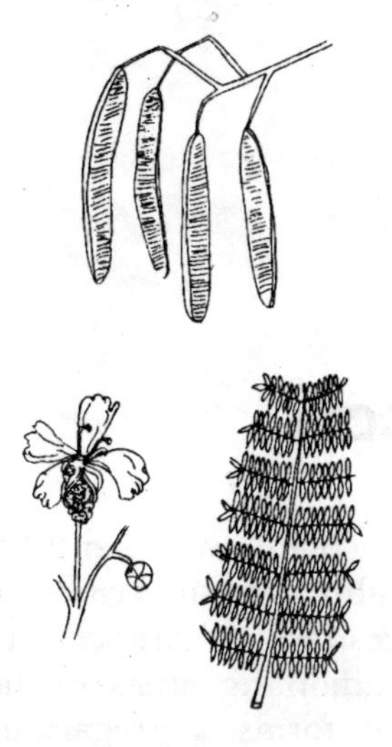

Delonix Regia

FLAMBOYANT

This is introduced specie that is now being grown successfully in the tropical and sub-tropical regions of the countries. They have been planted in lawns and along the roads in many states, as they are good landscaping trees. They are successful up to an elevation of 1000 m above sea level.

Botanical name of the tree is *Delonix regia,* Syn. *Poinciana regia* Bojer. and it belongs to family *Caesalpiniacea*. Vernacular name is Gulmohar.

Trees are deciduous in nature and may grow as high as 12 m with an equal spread under normal conditions. Canopy is spreading and becomes almost like an umbrella when the tree is full matured. Branching is not profuse but branches are wide and spreading. Trunk is knotty and strong with greyish brown bark, which is usually scaly.

Leaves are green, compound, feathery, long, bipinnate bearing 20 - 30 tiny leaflets.

Flowering is from April to June and then again in July-September. Flower colour is carmine to orange and very prominent

Fruits are pods, 30-45 cm long, flat, with brown skin. Pods twist on maturity to release the seeds.

Seeds are oblong to ovoid, yellowish marbled, brown and many in numbers in a single pod.

Trees are mostly planted for landscaping along the roads or in the centre of a lawn as they are fast growing avenue, ornamental or shade trees. Wood is soft and light that responds well to polishing.

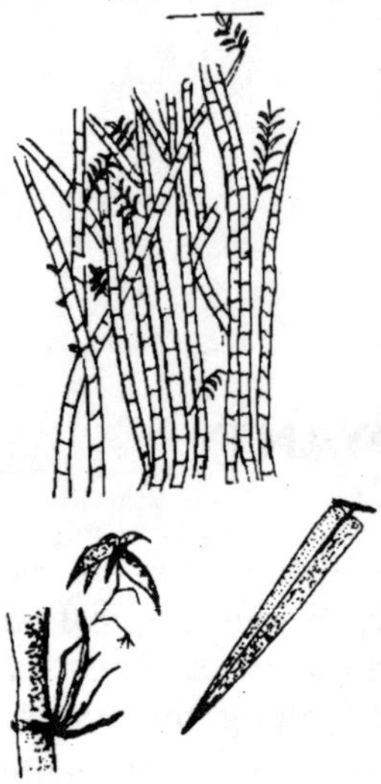

Dendrocalamus Strictus

BAMBOO

It is a valuable tree/plant for drier hills ascending upto 1200 m above mean sea level from Jammu, Himachal Pradesh, Uttaranchal to North Eastern Hills and adjoining areas in the outer Himalayas where it forms a gregarious clump.

Botanical name is *Dendrocalamus strictus* Nees for the species found in northern part while *Dendrocalamus hamiltonii* Nees and Arn. is for species found in eastern side, particularly Assam. These belong to the Family *Bambusaceae.* Vernacular name is Bans.

These are evergreen trees which may be 10-15 m long, underground stem known as rootstock is perennial and much branched which may be used for further propagation. Stem is green, erect, 5-10 cm in diameter, hollow from inside, rooting at joints (nodes) near the base nodes, which are swollen and yellowish in colour. Internodes may be 10-30 cm long, the internodal length decreases with height of the trunk.

Leaves are narrow, lanceolate, mid-rib prominent, finely pointed, 3-5 cm long.

Spikelets appear during winter in cooler years. 2-3 flowered, crowded in large, globose, sessile heads. Seeds are equal to the size of wheat grain and are edible.

Stems are used in a number of ways, mainly for building purposes and for masts of boats while section of the culms are used as buckets, flower pots, etc. Canes or thin shoots are used for sticks, and for mat and basket-making. Pulp may be used for manufacturing of paper. Twigs are used for pickling. Leaves are fed to cattle.

Diospyros Kaki

PERSIMMON

Commonly known as Japani Phal, is a fruit tree of mid-hills in the temperate region between the altitudinal ranges of 1000 m to 1500 m above mean sea level where regular rains are available while fruits are gaining size but there should be no frost during flowering.

Botanical name of persimmon is *Diospyros kaki* L. which belongs to Family *Ebenaceae*. These are deciduous and perennial trees growing to the height of 8 to 10 m with spread of about 6 m and assume conical crown on maturity. Bark is brown and cracked. Branching is strong, mostly horizontal with good crotch angles.

Leaves are entire, leathery and oval shaped, green, glossy on upper side but dull green and slightly rough on lower side, leaf stalk is 12-15 cm long.

Flowers are green, usually disguised among the leaves so are not visible from a distance.

Fruits are round to conical, green when immature but orange red on maturity, skin is glossy and may be edible along with pulp, hollow near the base, 5-6 cm across. Pulp is also yellowish red, sweet when ripe but astringent when unripe.

Seeds are small and do not mature when fruits are harvested. Some varieties are seedless.

Fruits are used in dessert when completely ripe. The nutritive value per 100 g of pulp is : moisture 80.0 g, protein 0.7 g, fat 0.2 g, mineral matter 0.3 g, fibre 0.9 g, carbohydrates 17.9 g, calcium 15 mg, phosphorus 10 mg, iron 0.3 mg, Vita A 1710 I.U., Thiamine 0.03 mg, Niacin in traces, Riboflavin 0.01 mg and Vita C 33 mg. Calorific value is 76 Kcal.

Wood is hard, elastic and very durable so used in doors for decoration.

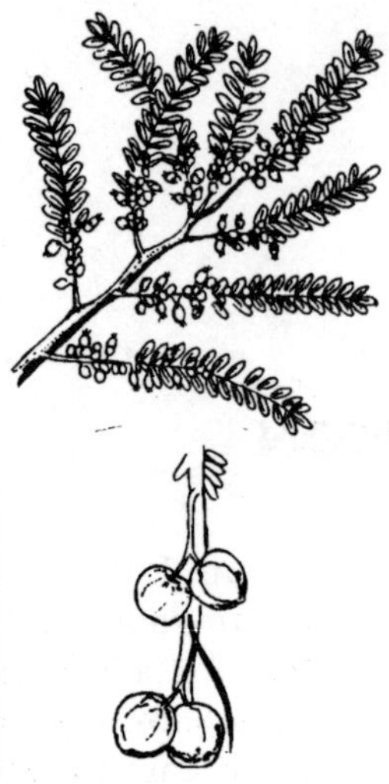

Emblica Officinalis

INDIAN GOOSEBERRY

These trees are found in outer Himalayas, mostly in the foothills of the western Himalayan region. Mostly drier slopes that have monsoon rains are rich with these trees. They are successfully raised up to 1000 m above mean sea level.

In the wild form, the trees are found to yield fruits of small size but rich in nutritive value, though yield less quantity of fruit, which are used in various medicinal preparations like Chvayanprash and Triphla (*Emblica officinalis, Terminalia bellirica* and *Terminalia chebula*).

Botanically Indian Gooseberry is *Emblica officinalis* Gaertn. belonging to the *Euphorbiaceae* Family. *Phyllanthus emblica* Linn. is synonym. In vernacular and common language, it is known as Aonla or Amla. Trees when grown for commercial purposes bear fruits which are used for making preserve, candy and pickle. Wild specie is referred as Kahu which is found in drier hills.

Trees are usually tall (20-30 m) and of medium spread (6-10 m) in forests but cultivated varieties are usually 8 m tall and 6 m in spread. Under cold climate, it may behave as deciduous. Main trunk is strong with light brown and scaly bark. Canopy is round but drooping.

Leaves are narrowly oblong, olive green, leaflets are 1-2 cm long and 0.5 cm wide, compounded.

Flowers, light green to pale green in colour are borne in bunches in axils of leaves during spring season.

Fruits are fleshy, capsular, smooth skinned, shining, olive or light green when fully developed but become greyish yellow on ripening.

Seed is light brown, hard, rigid, slightly round and two in each loculi.

Trees are grown for their fruits and leaves, which have high nutritive value and medicinal value. Fruits are acidic, astingent and rich source of Vita C and pectin. Wood is used for making handles of agricultural and other hand-tools. Fuel wood and fodder are also received from trees. Bark, leaves and fruits are used for tanning and dyeing.

Nutritive value of fruit is—81.8 g moisture, 0.5 g protein, 0.1 g fat, 0.5 g minerals, 3.4 g fibre, 13.7 g carbohydrates, 50 mg calcium, 20 mg phosphorous, 1-2 mg iron, Vita A 9 I.U., Thiamine 0.03 mg, Riboflavin 0.01 mg, Niacin 0.2 mg, Vita C 600 mg and energy released is 58 Kcal per 100 g of pulp.

Fruit is useful in therapy of hemorrhages, diarrhoea, dysentary, anemia, jaundice, dyspepsia and cough. It is also used for pickling and making preserve.

Eriobotrya Japonica

LOQUAT

Though trees of this species are best suited to the tropical and sub-tropical climate but they are being raised in hills and valley areas under the lap of the Himalayas in the Shiwalik ranges. Thus, they are seen almost in warm but humid areas.

Botanical name of the tree is *Eriobotrya japonica* Lind. and the family is *Rosaceae*. In vernacular, it is known as Loquat.

Trees are evergreen in nature and of moderate height, about 5-6 m with an equal spread. Trunk is strong, canopy is umbrella shaped with branches going mostly upwards. Bark is brownish grey and scaly.

Leaves are green, leathery, and glossy but have rust coloured tomentose on their lower surface. Margins are usually toothed, 15-25 cm x 4-6 cm with well-marked veins.

Flowers appear from September to February depending upon the region. They are white, sweet scented, small and borne in branched panicles that may have 40-100 flowers.

Fruits are conical to round in shape or pear shaped, golden yellow in colour with a soft to slightly rough skin that has a yellow pulp underneath. Pulp is acidic when half-ripe but sweet and juicy when full mature. Size is 4x5 cm with a green to brown stalk.

Seeds are large, 1 cm x 2 cm, brown, oblong to round, shining 2-3 in each fruit and are separable from the pulp.

Fruits are used as dessert fruits as they are aromatic, sweet with a fine blending of sugar and acidic taste. They have nutritive as well as medicinal value.

The nutritive value per 100 g of fresh pulp is—moisture 88.2 g, protein 0.6 g, fat 0.3 g, minerals 0.5 g, fibre 0.8 g, carbohydrates 9.6 g, calcium 30 mg, phosphorus 20 mg, iron 1.3 mg, Vita A 559 I.U., and calorific value is 43 Kcal.

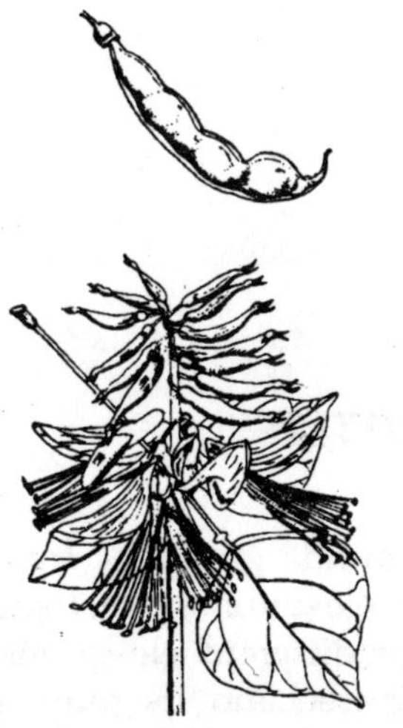

Erythrina Suberosa

CORAL TREE

The tree is found scattered throughout the greater part of the country in deciduous forests, particularly in the sub-Himalayan tract from Kashmir to Bhutan between elevation of 900 m to 1200 m. It is also found in cultivated areas.

Erythrina suberosa Roxb. is the botanical name and it belongs to Family *Papilionaceae*. In Hindi, the tree is known by the name of Pangra or Dhaudhak.

Trees are deciduous in nature. It is a medium sized tree about 12-15 m high with spiny, corky and deeply fissured bark and spreading branches. Branchlets are armed with sharp, stout, conical, whitish or light brown prickles.

Leaves are compound, 3 leaflets, broadly ovate, the terminal largest, 8-12 cm, all densely hairy beneath, often with reddish brown hairs and long stalked.

Flowers are showy, 5-10 cm, scarlet red in colour, appear just before or along with the young leaves in small short crowded clusters at the ends of the branches.

Pods are glabrous or hairless, cylindrical, long (10-12 cm), pointed, somewhat constricted between seeds, leathery and hard. 3-4 seeds in each pod.

Seeds are of dark purple colour.

Wood is very light, white, spongy but fibrous and tough and is used for making small articles, toys, etc. Leaves are lopped for fodder, which is reported to be of variable quality but not very good.

Eucalyptus

EUCALYPTUS

These trees are found growing from lower elevation to higher elevation since there are many species that suit different elevations. Since it is a fast growing tree and its pulp is used for manufacture of paper, packing cases, etc. is in demand and so is grown on all types of soils and under different climates.

Botanical name is *Eucalyptus* spp. and it belongs to Family *Myrtaceae*. In vernacular, it is known as Safaida since the bark of the tree is usually of white colour.

Generally, trees are evergreen in nature but they may behave as deciduous under cooler climate. Leaf fall is near complete as old leaves are replaced by new leaves in a short span.

Trees may attain the height of 15 to 20 m but they are kept low, about 10-12 m tall so that they may have a straight stem which is not very strong and is liable to break. Generally, they are kept as single stemmed but they branch haphazardly. Bark is papery and pink to grey in colour, which may peel off in patches.

Foliage is olive green, 10 x 3 cm, aromatic and sparse, mid-rib is quite prominent, long petioled, pointed on both ends.

Flowers are white, aromatic and almost invisible from a distance.

Fruits are odd shaped capsules, brown in colour and woody.

Seeds are small.

Wood is not of very good quality, hence used for poles, pulp is used for manufacture of paper and for match-industry, packing cases and charcoal. Timber is strong and straight. Scented oil obtained from the tree is used in various medical and pharmaceutical preparations. Trees are used as wind-breaks. Bees prefer the flowers as they have a nectar.

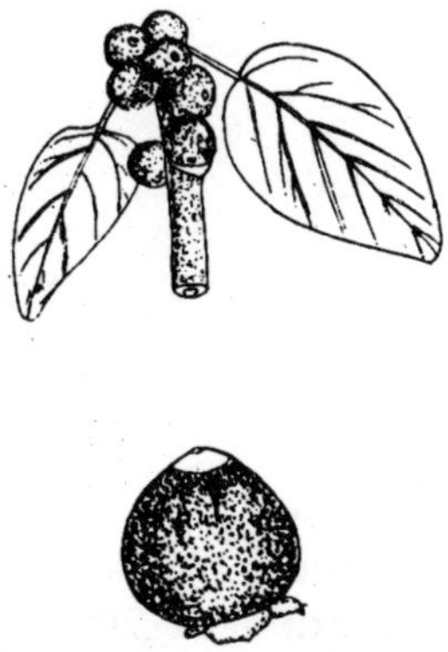

Ficus Benghalensis

BANYAN

It is a majestic tree found growing up to 1500 m above mean sea level in outer Himalayas in the areas from Pakistan to Assam in almost all the States. Trees are also seen in Southern hilly areas and plains of the country. Trees are quite hardy and can withstand temperature upto 48°C during summer. They grow best when the annual rainfall is within the range of 500-4000 mm.

Botanical name of the species is *Ficus benghalensis* Linn. and this belongs to the Family *Moraceae*. Banyan is commonly known as Bargad, Barh or Borh in vernacular.

Trees are evergreen in nature, going as high as 20-25 m with an equal spread in all directions. Main trunk is short but branches are dense with a spreading crown. Bark is light brown to dark brown. Branches send aerial roots which establish and help the branches to spread further.

Leaves are leathery, green, 10-12 cm x 5-10 cm, obtuse, entire, stalk is round and 1-3 cm long and thick.

Flowers appear during summer.

Fruit is a composite fig, red when ripe, 1-2 cm across, round, hairy, axillary and edible.

Seeds are dark brown, small and many in a fruit.

Trees are raised as avenue and shade trees. Mostly found near temples, roadside and in common places. They have medicinal value. Leaves are fed to elephants. Tree as a whole is regarded as a sacred tree as it is worshipped by many communities in India.

Ficus Carica

FIG

The trees of this species are found scattered on the marginal lands, wastelands and boundaries upto an elevation of 2000 m asml. At higher altitudes, fruits do not ripen and they remain of small size. It is scattered from Afghanistan to Uttaranchal and is also found in South of country.

Botanical name is *Ficus carica* Linn. and belongs to Family *Moraceae*. In vernacular, it is known as Anjeer.

It is a small tree that may be 3-4 m tall and of same spread but is deciduous in cooler region and may retain some leaves in lower elevations. Bark is greenish pink. Root system is extensive. Branchlets and leaves are hairy on the lower side. Branching is upright and later spreading.

Leaves are quite big, 6-8 cm x 5-6 cm in size, 3-5 lobed, dark green, leathery, slightly succulent and borne on long stalks, upper surface is smooth while dorsal surface is slightly rough and less green in colour than the upper surface, dentate margins with irregular teeth.

Flowers appear during spring or early summer in groups, green, pear shaped and bloom for a short period.

Fruits are pear shaped, conical, 3-4 cm x 1.5 cm, dark brown, purple or greenish purple to yellow. Fruit is aggregate.

Seeds are usually rudimentary, small and papery.

Fruits are valued for their nutritive and medicinal value. They are used both when fresh and dried. Jam, candy and preservers are prepared. Leaves are used for making plates.

100 g fruit may contain 88.1 g moisture, 12.3 g protein, 0.2 g fat, 0.6 g mineral matter, 80 mg calcium, 30 mg phosphorus, 1.0 mg iron, Vita A 162 I.U., Thiamine 0.06 mg, Riboflavin 0.05 mg, Niacin 0.6 mg, Vita C 5 mg and provide 37 Kcal energy.

Ficus Glomerata

GULAR

It is a characteristic tree of the tropical hill valley swamp forests found around Dehradun and like areas of Uttaranchal and Himachal Pradesh in the sub-Himalayan tract and outer Himalayan valleys. It is also available in Rajasthan, Bihar, West Bengal, Khasi Hills, Madhya Pradesh, Maharashtra, etc.

Ficus glomerata Roxb. belongs to Family *Moraceae.* Ficus is the Latin name while Gular or Guler is the Hindi name.

Trees are evergreen but they behave as deciduous since old leaves are shed during winter and new leaves appear soon after. It is a moderate to large sized tree, often going as high as 18 m, with a short bole and spreading crown and without aerial roots as other members of the family have. Bark is reddish brown, smooth with large cracks.

Leaves, entire, elongate-elliptic ovate or elliptic lanceolate, base acute or rounded and 7-10 cm long.

Fruits are clustered on leafless branches, globose or pear shaped 2.5 cm to 4.0 cm in diameter and are edible. They mature from March to July.

Seeds are many but small.

Leaves are lopped for fodder, which is of fairly good quality. Gum is also extracted. Fruits are edible. They have a thick syrup. Wood is not very durable so used for rough purposes. It is regarded as a sacred tree since it is believed that near every Gular tree, there runs a hidden stream.

Ficus Religiosa

PIPAL

Though this specie is of the tropical origin but is found growing in the sub-tropical region and temperate region also under the Himalayan ranges up to an elevation of 1400 m above mean sea level in moist areas, particularly in valleys and lower hills. It is most common in Central India and Bengal region. Being a sacred tree, it is planted near religious places, on community lands and near water ponds, roads and paths.

Trees belong to the Family *Moraceae* and the botanical name is *Ficus religiosa* Linn. These are deciduous but leaf-fall is for a very short period in hot weather.

Trees are quite large and spreading, often 20 m tall and 10 m in spread. Crown is round. Branches are mostly upright, later drooping and spreading. Bark is papery and greyish pink in colour, which peels off to give place for the new one.

Leaves are leathery, broadly ovate, 12 cm long with long petiole and a long tail like tip, a remarkable fashion that forms a cuspidate appendix. Young leaves are pink but they become green on expansion and are shining on the upper surface while lower surface is hairy or slightly rough. Veins are prominent. Leaf size may be 12 cm x 8 cm.

Male flowers are few.

Fruits are small, 0.5 to 0.75 cm across, almost globose, sessile, in pairs in axils of leaves, purple, ripen in summer and edible.

Seeds are small and many in a single fruit.

It is a sacred tree of Hindus and Buddhists and is mostly planted near templs, ponds and other common places. It is used as an avenue, ornamental, shade, medicinal and multipurpose tree.

TRIMLA

Trees grow in the sub-Himalayan tract ascending in the outer Himalayas upto an elevation of about 1800 m in hills from Jammu-Kashmir to Manipur. Trees are of sub-tropical region and are mostly in moist places along streams or moist areas.

Botanical name of this specie is *Ficus roxburghii* Wall. This plant belongs to Family *Moraceae, Ficus auriculata* Lour. and *Ficus macrophylla* Roxb. are synonyms.

Trees are spreading and deciduous in nature but remain leafless for a short period during December-January when there is winter. It is a spreading tree with grey warty bark. Old leaves start falling in late autumn and new leaves appear in early spring, i.e. February-March. Young shoots are velvety. Trunk is erect but crooked when mature, crown is broad. Trees become bushy with short stem and spreading crown.

Leaves are stalked, green, broadly ovate, 20 cm x 15 cm, entire or dentate, base deeply cordate and sometimes rounded.

Flowering takes place in March.

Fruiting starts in April-May. Fruits are depressed turbinate, 3-5 cm long and 5-7 cm in diameter, longitudinally ribbed, hairy, russet brown or purple when ripe. They mature in April-May.

Leaves are lopped for fodder, which is fairly palatable and digestible. Fruits are edible. Bark produces fibre which is used for rope making. Wood is durable and is used for making walking sticks and pastles.

INDIAN ASH TREE

It is one of the tree of Ash group which is found growing from Himachal Pradesh to South West China within the altitudinal range of 1200-2700 m asml in forests planted around villages. It is also found in Khasi Hills. In some tribes it is regarded as a sacred tree.

Botanical name is *Fraxinus floribunda* Wallich, *Syn. F. nicrantha* Ling. and belongs to family *Oleaceae.* Another spp. *F. micrantha* Ling. is very similar to this and is found in Kumaon and Shimla Hills.

It is deciduous in nature so sheds the leaves during autumn or early winter. Trees are large in size. Bark is grey and smooth on young trees, rough and longitudinally furrowed on older trees. Leafless during winter, branchlets are purple.

Leaves are odd-pinnate with 7-9 elliptic-lanceolate, long, pointed, saw toothed, stalked leaflets, 6-10 cm long, hairy beneath.

Numerous white flowers, which are large, 25 cm long, are borne in branched clusters. Flowers appear during summer.

Fruit is with a long or wide narrow wing, 1-seeded nut, 2.5 cm to 4 cm long, 3-4 mm broad with blunt or notched apex.

Wood is used for making poles, oars and ploughs. It is pinkish white, moderately hard and tough. Trees are planted for ornamentation.

Grevillea Robusta

SILVER OAK

Plantations of this species are found ascending upto 2300 m above mean sea level as the trees are able to tolerate temperature down to minus 10°C and can withstand drought. Being hardy have found place at different locations and pockets.

They belong to the Family *Proteaceae* and the botanical name is *Grevillea robusta* A. Cunn.

Tree are graceful and deciduous in nature. Main trunk is clean and cylindrical, height may be 20 m or so with a spread of 8 m. Spreading crown.

Foliage is finely cut and silvery grey beneath looking best when disturbed by wind hence the name as Silver Oak. Leaves are bipinnatifid, like a big fern, green on upper side but silvery below.

Inflorescence is raceme on old wood of the previous year. Flowers are apetalous with a short calyx of 4 upturned lobes, orange, small in clusters.

Fruits are follicles with 1-2 flat winged seeds, ripe during winter.

Seed, one or two in each follicle.

Flowers are very attractive to bees, making this as an important honey plant. Trees are good as avenue, shade and road-side plantation. Fuel and timber are also used. It grows fast and looks attractive for about 10-15 years and later looks rugged.

BIUL

It is a common tree that grows in the Himalayas from Jammu and Kashmir to Nepal up to 2000 m above mean sea level. Trees do not occur in forest but are seen as a part of the social-forestry plantation along the agricultural fields and other places.

Biul is known by other names like Bihul, Bhimal, Dhaman, etc. It belongs to Family *Tiliaceae* and its botanical name is *Grewia optiva* Drummond. It is a middle-sized tree, evergreen, 5 to 6 m tall and 4-5 m in spread. Canopy is spreading.

New leaves emerge during spring after shedding of old leaves and as such trees may be leafless for a week or 10 days. Flowers also appear soon after the expansion of leaves.

Fruits are fleshy drupe, olive green, which later become blackish and have scattered hairs. These ripe during October to December. It is a fleshy drupe and is 2-4 lobed.

Seed has a hard seedcoat.

Trees can grow on a variety of soils, but they need irrigation for quality fodder. It is also a sub-tropical tree, which grows well in valleys and mid-hills where temperature does not exceed 38°C during summer and does not drop below 2°C during winter.

Biul tree is raised for fodder, timber and fuel. A single tree may yield 12-15 kg of green fodder, which is available during winter months. Leaves contain 19.05 per cent crude protein, 18.0 per cent crude fibre, 3.0 per cent calcium and 0.15 per cent phosphorus. Wood is fairly hard and is used for making handles of agricultural tools. Leaves contain tannin to some extent and are used for tanning.

Jacaranda Mimosifolia

JACARANDA

These trees are found growing along the roads, paths and in centre of lawns in the mid-hills, valleys and other areas falling in the altitudinal range upto 1600 m above mean sea level in the hills of Jammu-Kashmir, Himachal Pradesh, Uttaranchal and other parts of sub-Himalayan tract.

Botanical name of the tree is *Jacaranda mimosifolia* D. Don which is synonym to *J. acutifolia* and it belongs to Family *Bignoniaceae.*

Trees are deciduous in nature and the height may go up to 15 m or so with a spread of about 8 m. Trunk is strong and straight. Branching is upright and open but on appearance of flowers, they become pendulous. Canopy is oval. Bark is brownish grey.

Leaves are compound, petioled, finely cut fern like leaflets, which may be 40-100 in number, green, small and oval.

Bloom is in the form of loose pyramidal terminal panicles, numbering 40-100 flowers appear during March-May and is of blue-mauve colour.

Fruit is an oblong, dehiscent and woody capsule.

Seeds are papery, brown and winged.

Trees are ornamental and shady in nature. Wood is not of very good quality but is used for making furniture and other petty handles.

Juglans Regia

WALNUT

It is a native of north-western Himalayas and as such are found growing here and there in many parts where they do not get spring frost, summers are normal and there is enough chill during winter to keep the tree under dormancy for at least 2.5 months.

There is no organized plantation of walnut trees but they are found scattered in the mid and high hill areas in the region particularly, Jammu-Kashmir, Himachal Pradesh, Uttaranchal and North-Eastern States.

Walnut trees are deciduous in nature and belong to Family *Juglandaceae*, the botanical name being *Juglans regia* L. Vernacular name is Akhrot. Trees are strong stemmed, almost 15 m tall with a spread of 8 m or so. Branching is strong and spreading with good crotch angles. Canopy is round. Bark is usually dark brown.

Leaves are compound, large and green with the upper surface having shine.

Flowers of brownish green colour appear in early spring.

Fruits are round to oval, hard skinned/shelled having kernel in the centre and are 3-4 cm long. Fruits are harvested during summer and then dried under shade and sun. They remain good for one season.

Fruits are nutritious, 100 g having 4-5% moisture, 64.5 g fat, 15.6 g protein, 11.0 g carbohydrates, 2.6 g fibre, 1.8 g mineral matter, 100 mg calcium, 380 mg phosphorus, 2.64 mg iron, 1.0 mg Niacin, 0.45 mg Thiamine and 0.40 mg Riboflavin. Fruits are also rich in Vita B (6 ug) and have Calorific value of 687 Kcal per 100 g.

It is an ornamental, aromatic, avenue, shade and fruit tree which is also planted on borders and humid areas.

Trees are valued for their fruits, which are used for extraction of oil, and dry fruit, bark for tanning and medicinal purpose while the wood is of prime quality.

Trees are slow growing in the initial stages and take more than ten years to bear fruits and hence people do not prefer to plant these trees. This is due to the myth among the local people, which has not encouraged their planting. Only aged persons plant these trees since there is a belief that a person who plants the walnut tree may not live long. Trees come to fruiting after 10-15 years.

Juniperus Macropoda

PENCIL CEDAR

Commonly known as Juniper, which is found growing from Pakistan to Uttaranchal through Jammu-Kashmir and Himachal Pradesh in the altitudinal range between 2400 m to 4300 m in the dry river valleys, forms a gregarious tree.

This species belongs to Family *Cupressaceae* and its botanical name is *Juniperus macropoda* Boiss. The trees are evergreen in nature. Tree height may be 18 m or so. Branching is upright.

Leaves are sharp and pointed on lower branches and scale like on the upper branches and branchlets. Lower leaves are linear, 8 mm, scale leaves 1.5 cm, closely pressed to stem with a large resinous gland on the back.

Fruit has 2 or more, bluish black, resinous seeds.

Wood is most suitable for furniture making, building and pencil making. Since it is used for pencils hence its name Pencil Cedar. Wood is also used for fuel and charcoal making.

Lagerstroemia Parviflora

DHAURA/DHAURI

Trees are found scattered in the sub-Himalayan tract from the Yamuna River eastward ascending up to 800 m elevation. It is common in the lower hills of Uttaranchal.

Botanical name is *Lagerstroemia parviflora* Roxb. and it belongs to Family *Lythraceae*.

Trees are deciduous and of moderate size, and may attain large size if raised under congenial conditions. Young parts are usually glabrous. Bark is light grey in colour, thin, smooth, exfoliating in narrow longitudinal flakes/strips.

Leaves opposite, 6.4-12.7 cm x 2.5-5.0 cm, narrowly elliptic, young leaves hairy beneath, mature leaves glabrous on both sides. Leaves are shed in February and new leaves appear in April.

Flowers appear during summer. They are white, fragrant and borne in terminal panicles.

Fruits ripen in winter from December to February, capsules, brown and are 3 or 4 valved.

Seeds are brown with a papery wing and a thick stiff curved ridge along one edge.

Tree is lopped for fodder, especially for buffaloes. Timber is used for building construction as posts, beams, rafters, etc., and also for hand-tools, agricultural implements, carts, oars, furniture, fuel and charcoal.

JHINGAN

These trees are found throughout the greater part of the country in mixed deciduous forests. These are found growing up to 1300 m elevation in the sub-Himalayan tract and valleys.

Botanical name is *Lannea coromandelica (*Houtt.) Merr. and Syn. is *L. grandis* (Dennst.) Engl. It belongs to Family *Anacardiaceae.* It is known by the name Jigma, Kaimal, Ginjan, etc. in Hindi.

Trees are deciduous in nature, moderate to large in size with spreading crowns and stout branches, attaining height of 24 m or so. Bark is thick, grey and smooth in young trees, exfoliating in thin irregular plates in old trees. Sapwood is white.

Leaves are imparipinnate, leaflets 3-4 pairs, opposite and entire. Old leaves fall in winter and the tree remains leafless for 2-3 months and even more. New leaves appear in early summer.

Flowering takes place during February to April depending on the climate and are yellowish or purple in colour.

Fruit is a drupe, remiform, oblong and about 1.0 cm to 1.5 cm long with a hard stone. They ripen during summer, i.e. May-June.

Wood is used for different purposes like making packing cases, furniture, yokes, oil press, rice pounder, plough, shafts, etc. Leaves are lopped for fodder, which is of good quality. Bark, leaves and gum have medicinal use. Leaves are boiled and applied for relieving local swelling and pain from body.

Litchi Chinensis

LITCHI

Trees of litchi are found growing in sub-tropical areas, which are mild and have plenty of rains during the rainy season but not when the fruits are maturing as rains at that time causes splitting of fruits and uneven ripening. Most of the areas in the outer Himalayas lying in the lower hills and valleys have trees of litchi. Nainital, Udham Singh Nagar, Dehradun, Dhaula Kuan, Nagrota, Nupur and other areas of Dhauladhar range are famous for raising of these trees. Some plantations have also come up in Jammu area and Punjab.

It is an evergreen tree, botanically known as *Litchi chinensis* Son. belonging to Family *Sapindaceae*. Trees are of moderate height (8-10 m long). Canopy is spreading, round to slightly umbrella type. Bark is brown and slightly scaly. Branches are strong but spreading.

Leaves are in pairs of 2-4 leaflets, oblong to lanceolate, green, glossy above and glaucous below, 10 cm x 5 cm with pointed tips and a round but green petiole.

Whitish flowers appear in spring season.

Fruits are round to oval or conical, 2.5 cm x 1.5 cm, borne in clusters with a long stalk, pericarp is woody and brown to pinkish red in colour. Portion between pericarp and seed is aril which is edible, white, sweet, smelling, juicy and 0.5-0.75 cm thick surrounding the brown coloured seed which is egg-shaped, 1 cm x 1.5 cm and even some varieties may have rudimentary seed.

Trees are mostly raised for their delicious and juicy fruits, which are sweet with a peculiar smell and taste. Fruits can be preserved in syrup, processed into squash, drink, etc. Leaves are used for decoration while wood is semi-hard and used for domestic purposes.

The nutritive value of fruit as measured for 100 g of pulp is—84.3 g moisture, 0.3 g fat, 0.7 g protein, 2.25 g fibre, 9.4 g carbohydrates, 0.7 g minerals including 0.21 g calcium, 0.31 g phosphorus and 0.03 g iron, 14 I.U. Vita A, 87.5 mg Thiamine, 122.5 mg Riboflavin. Calorific value is 42 Kcal.

Madhuca Indica

MAHUA

It is a tree of the deciduous forests of central, western and south eastern parts of the country and extending north to the sub-Himalayan tract.

Botanical name of the tree is *Madhuca indica* J. Gmel. and is synonym to *Madhuca latifolia* (Roxb.) Maebride belonging to Family *Sapotaceae*.

Trees are deciduous in nature, large 15-20 m tall, with spreading branches but having stout and small trunk, canopy is round. Bark is blackish grey with vertical cracks.

New leaves appear in May which are coppery red in colour while old leaves are shed during winter. Leaves are leathery and cluster near the tips of shoots.

Flowers appear during spring, just prior to leaves, cream coloured, 1 cm across.

Fruits ripen from June to August, berry, juicy and are edible.

Seeds are small, cream or copper coloured, smooth and shining.

Trees are raised by seeds and the saplings are transplanted when one year old.

Trees are cultivated for their flowers and fruits, flowers are eaten raw or cooked or dried, ground and mixed with flour, or distilled. Trees also provide shade. Oil is extracted from seeds, which is used for cooking, lighting and for soap industry. Bark is used as a dye. Milky juice is used as a medicine. Wood is of good quality and is used for manufacture of furniture, boats, and many other items of use.

Ripe Mahua fruit contains 73.6 g moisture, 1.4 g protein, 1.6 g fat, 0.7 g mineral matter, 22.7 g carbohydrates, 45 mg calcium, 22 mg phosphorus, .023 mg iron and calorific value is 111 Kcal per 100 g of edible portion.

Mallotus Philippinensis

ROHINI

Trees are found in almost throughout the country ascending to 1500 m above mean sea level in the hills right from Pakistan to Assam. These grow best in the valleys along the Sutlej and Giri Valleys of Himachal Pradesh, Shivalik and outer Himalaya in the moist areas.

Botanical name is *Mallotus philippinensis* (L.) Muell. Arg. and this belongs to the Family *Euphorbiaceae*. Trees are not large but usually are pubescent.

Leaves alternate, long stalked, variable in form, usually ovate or ovate-lanceolate, 7-13 cm, entire or sinuate, upper surface glabrous, lower rusty tomentose, minutely scarlet-dotted.

Flowers are small in panicled racemes or spikes, the male and female are on different trees. Male flowers are yellowish, shortty stalked, usually 3 together in slender drooping racemes, which is 7-15 cm long. Female flowers are solitary, sessile, in stiff nearly erect spikes, which are 5-7 cm long.

Fruit is a capsule, globose, 1 cm in diameter, 3 lobed, covered with a bright red powder.

Seeds are 3 in each capsule, black and smooth.

Powder over the fruits is collected for dyeing silk and used in medicines.

Malus Domestica

APPLE

Apple is an important fruit crop of the western Himalayas. It is extensively grown in various parts of Shimla, Kullu, Kinnaur, Sirmaur, Chamba and Mandi districts of Himachal Pradesh: higher reaches in Jammu and mid-hills to higher hills in Kashmir and under mid-hills and high hills of Uttaranchal. Plantations have also come up in North-Eastern States and hills in South India.

Trees are seen both in planned orchards and scattered on contours under temperate climate where they get temperature below 4°C during winter for 1000 hours and 20°-28°C during summer for 60 days or so. It has become a commercial crop due to heavy economic returns to the growers.

Apple belongs to Family *Rosaceae* and its botanical name is *Malus domestica*. Local name is Seb. It is deciduous in nature. Other strains of *Malus* specie are also found in some parts, which are good as pollinizers and rootstocks.

Trees usually attain the height of over 10 m and spread of 8 m on seedlings but grafted trees remain 6-7 m tall and 5 m in spread.

Leaves are slightly leathery, elliptical, serrate, dark green above and light green on dorsal side, 10x4 cm, petioled, young leaves are light green. They appear slightly before flowers.

Trees start blooming during spring, which lasts for 7-10 days. Bloom is of pink colour, which turns white after 3 days. Flowering is profuse in bunches of 5 flowers. These are slightly scented, which attracts the honeybees and other insects and this helps/boosts the pollination.

Leaves are shed after harvest of fruits in September-October and trees remain leafless till the end of winter season.

Fruits of different shapes and colours (according to variety) are borne in clusters but thinned to have one fruit at one place. Fruits are harvested carefully by manual labour during the end of June to September (season vary according to place). Fruits are usually round to oblong, red or yellow, 10 cm x 8 cm, stalked, sweet smelling and fairly hard with a shining surface.

Fruits are liked by everyone being nutritive and refreshing. The nutritive value per 100 g of fresh fruit is—moisture 84.6 g, fat 0.5 g, protein 0.2 g, mineral matter 0.3 g, fibre 1.0 g, carbohydrates 13.4 g, calcium 10 mg, phosphorus 14 mg, iron 0.7 mg, magnesium 7 mg, sodium 20 mg, potassium 75 mg, sulphur 7 mg, Thiamine 0.12 mg, Riboflavin 0.30 mg, Niacin 0.20 mg, Vita C 2 mg, Calorific value is 59 Kcal.

Mangifera Indica

MANGO

Mango trees are being grown in this country since ages in many parts of the country, starting from the coastal areas to lower hills or valleys.

Trees are highly sensitive to frost and are killed by frost; young trees are killed while old trees are severely injured. Their plantation is limited to lower areas and valleys where the spring frost is mild and summers are hot. Trees are seen in clusters and as scattered trees along the roadside and near water courses.

It belongs to the Family *Anacardiaceae* and the botanical name is *Mangifera indica* Linn. Vernacular name is Aam or Amb.

Under good conditions, the trees are about 15-20 m tall with spread of 10 m. Vegetative propagated trees are usually round about 10 m x 10 m. Bark is dark brown and splitting when mature. Branching is strong.

Leaves are green, large and glossy on upper surface while hairy on lower side, new flesh of leaves is red and smooth.

Flowers are borne in large panicles having thousands of yellowish green flowers which appear in February or so.

Fruits vary in shape, size, and colour, juicy, sweet, slighty to highly aromatic with a papery to large seedstone in the centre surrounded by fibrous or smooth pulp of yellow colour.

Fruits can be hand picked or removed by a shear along with small stalk. On harvesting, there is a bleeding of latex from the cut end which dries up soon. It is a cash crop of plains and lower hilly areas.

Nutritive value of pulp per 100 g of ripe mango is—moisture 81.0 g, protein 0.6 g, fat 0.4 g, mineral matter 0.4 g, fibre 0.7 g, carbohydrates 16.9 g, calcium 14 mg, phosphorus 16 mg, iron 1.3 mg, magnesium 270 mg, sodium 26 mg, potassium 205 mg, Vita A 4800 I.U., Thiamine 0.4 mg, Riboflavin 0.3 mg, Niacin 0.50 mg, Vita C 13 mg, and Calorific value is 74 Kcal.

Generally seedling trees are raised, which yield fruits of smaller size with much juice and less pulp, which is mostly fibrous. These are used for sucking or making mango leather. Raw or green fruits are used for pickling, chutney making, for candy, preserve and mango powder. Seed stones are used as substitute for food.

Wood is used for making packing cases, agricultural tools and domestic articles. Leaves are used for decoration, worship and for medicinal purposes. It is an evergreen tree with lush green foliage and huge round canopy underneath which normally no vegetation is found.

Melia Azedarach

BEAD TREE

Tree is indigenous to Kashmir but is found growing in many parts of the country. In Himalayas, it grows upto an elevation of about 1800 m above means sea level. Trees are seen along roadsides and villages but best are under valley areas having moderate heat in the North-West Himalayas.

It is also known as Bakain and Drake. Its botanical name is *Melia azedarach* Linn. which belongs to Family *Meliaceae*. It is deciduous in nature.

Trees are of moderate height (10-12 m). Branches are spreading to provide a round canopy. Trunk is short with a small bole. Bark is dark grey and vertically fissured having furrows. Branches are weak.

Leaves are green, twice pinnate, with several pairs of ovate-acuminate leaflets with toothed margins, leaflets 3-12, pointed, 1.5 to 4 cm long. New leaves appear during spring.

Flowers are borne in panicles of lilac colour, axillary, long stalked, 7-9 mm long. These appear along with new leaves during spring.

Fruit is globular or ovoid, drupe, 1.5 cm across, yellowish when ripe, borne in clusters, smooth and seeded. Young fruits i.e., fresh fruits are smooth but they get wrinkles on maturity, even on the tree as they can hang for a long period even after complete leaffall. Fruit is usually 5 seeded and has a hard endocarp.

Tree has medicinal value, as leaves, young fruits, bark and seeds are used in various medicinal uses. The fleshy part of the fruit has an unpleasant smell, especially when ripe. Gum is also extracted. Seeds known as beads are used to make necklace. Leaves are lopped for fodder. Wood quality is poor so used mostly for fuel purpose but furniture is also made. Oil is extracted from fruits.

Trees are ornamental, shady and fast growing but short-lived.

CHAMPA

Trees are found in eastern Himalayas, northeast India and Western Ghats but are cultivated throughout India for their fragrance. They are best suited for moist tropical regions.

Botanical name of the specie is *Michelia champaca* Linn. and it belongs to Family *Magnoliaceae.*

It is an evergreen tree usually 30 m in height and 3.5 m in girth, with a clean cylindrical bole up to 20 m long. Bark is of grey or brownish colour and smooth.

Leaves are ovate to lanceolate coriaceous.

Flowers are usually axillary solitary, yellow or orange and fragrant and appear in summer and monsoon.

Fruits are 5-10 cm long.

Seeds are brown, angular with pink fleshy aril, oily and lose viability soon.

Almost all the parts of tree have medicinal use. Root and root bark are used as purgatives. Flowers and fruits are considered stimulant, antisparmodic and tonic. Seeds and fruits are used for healing cracks in feet. Wood is used for posts, boards, veneers, furniture, decorative fillings, etc. Trees are good for soil conservation.

Mimusops elengi

INDIAN MEDLER

Trees are found in sub-tropical and tropical humid areas in the Indian Peninsula along the Western Ghats from Mumbai southwards and on the east from the Northern Circars southwards. It is also found in the Andamans in the evergreen and semi-deciduous forests.

Vernacular name of the specie is *Maulsari* and Botanical name is *Mimusops elengi* Linn, belonging to family *Sopotaceae.*

It is an evergreen tree, which may be medium to large in size with a dense crown of shining leathery leaves of waxy margin. Branches are spreading providing the tree a canopy of umbrella to crown shape, bark is dark grey and scaly.

Leaves are thick, flat, narrow, green, 2 cm x 3 cm, pointed at the tips.

Flowers are fragrant, white to dull white, star shaped, which appear during the spring season.

Fruits are smooth, berry, green during initial stages but turn red on maturity and are pulpy.

Seed is small and one in each fruit.

Trees are raised as ornamental trees and for the sake of their fragrant flowers which are used for making garlands and for distilling into perfume. Wood is hard, dark red, heavy, strong and durable and is used for many purposes. Fruit is edible and seeds yield an oil used for lighting, cooking, etc.

Morus alba

MULBERRY

Trees are found growing in almost all types of climate, as they are well suited to different agro-climatic conditions. It is found from Jammu and Kashmir to Assam, which includes the States like Himachal Pradesh, Uttaranchal and others. In the Himalayas, it ascends upto an elevation of about 1200 m. These are found in moist and slightly shady areas so that they can grow nicely. Trees are also found in valley and lower hills of other hilly States.

Botanical name of the tree is *Morus alba* Linn. and it belongs to Family *Moraceae.* In Hindi, it is known as Shehtoot or Toot. It is deciduous in nature. Old leaves are shed during November-December and the trees remain leafless during winter. The new leaves appear during early spring season.

Trees are moderate in size, about 6-10 m tall with a spread of about 6 m. Crown is spreading. Bole is clean. Branching is strong but slender. Bark is smooth during early period of growth but becomes rough on old or mature trees. It is brownish grey in colour.

Leaves are green, 7-10 cm across, long petioled, simple, alternate, acute, cordate, often three lobed, glabrous to scabrous, smooth with a channelled petiole.

Flowers are unisexual in catkins.

Fruit is a composite berry, which may be of white, cream, pink, purple or dark brown colour. Shape may be round or cylindrical. Generally round ones are 1 cm across while the cylindrical ones are less than one cm across but 4-5 cm long : juicy, sweet, slightly scented. They ripen from April to June.

Seeds are very small and brown in colour.

Nutritive value of fresh fruits per 100 gm is—moisture 86.5 g, protein 1.1 g, fat 0.4 g, minerals 0.6 g, fibre 1.1 g, carbohydrates 103 g, calcium 70 mg, phosphorus 30 mg, iron 2.3 mg, Vita A 57 I.U., Thiamine 0.04 mg, Riboflavin 0.13 mg, Niacin 0.5 mg, Vita C 12 mg, and energy is 49 Kcal.

It is a multipurpose tree that serves many purposes like fuel wood, canes for making baskets, wood for making handles of agricultural implements and hand tools and frames. Leaves are used as fodder for cattle and for raising of silk worms. Fruits are eaten. The tree provides shade and is good as avenue, roadside plantation, etc.

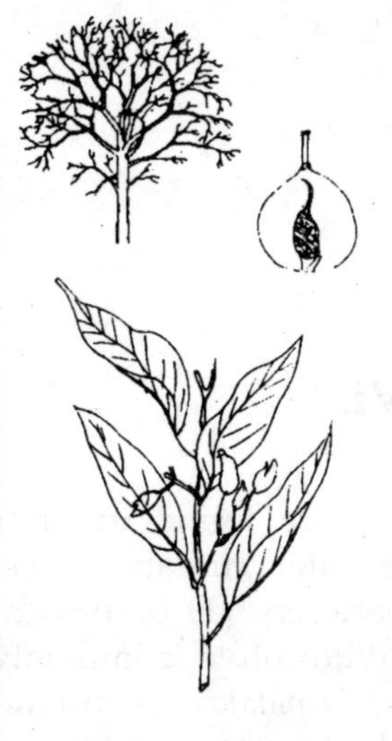

Myristica Fragrans

NUTMEG

The tree is found growing in tropical and sub-tropical regions where humid climate is available.

Botanical name of the specie is *Myristica fragrans* and it belongs to Family *Myristiceae.* In vernacular, it is known as Jaiphal.

Trees are moderately tall, about 10-15 m in height with sufficient spread and are deep rooted.

.Leaves are alternate, oval with short petiole, dark green on the upper side while light green on the dorsal side and aromatic.

Flowers are small, yellowish or greenish yellow, dioecious, male flowers have a number of stamens joined in a little column while female flowers have a single carpel. Both are scented.

Fruit is a fleshy pear shaped berry, which opens on ripening to release the seeds.

One seed in each fruit, seed is surrounded by a fibrous aril which changes from reddish to yellowish brown when dried, oval 1.5 cm x 0.5 cm.

Tree has a medicinal value. Mace is used in cooking and perfumery while the bare seed treated with lime is the nutmeg and is used to flavour food and drinks and is of medicinal value.

Nutmeg fruit contains per 100 g, 14.3 g moisture, 7.5 g protein, 36.4 g fat, 1.7 g mineral matter, 11.6 g fibre, 28.5 g carbohydrates, 120 mg calcium, 240 mg phosphorus, 2.03 mg iron, 229 mg magnesium, 0.71 mg copper, 1.78 mg manganese, 1.22 mg zinc, 0.234 mg chromium, 0.33 mg Thiamine, 0.01 mg Riboflavin, 1.4 mg Niacin and provides 472 Kcal energy.

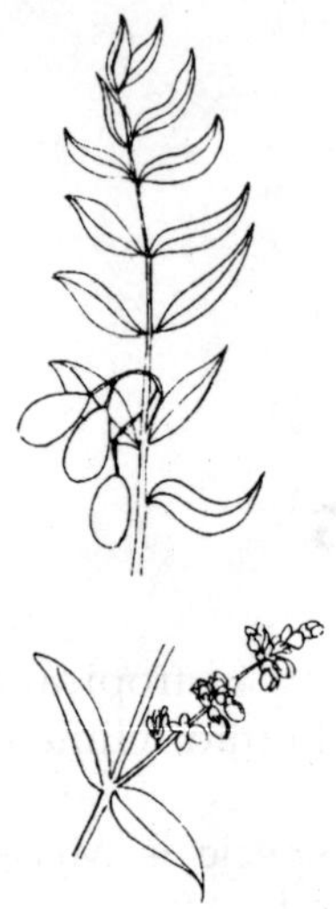

Olea Europaea

OLIVE

Trees of this species are found in drier hills in the middle of the outer Himalayas, i.e. in the altitudinal range between 600 to 1000 m above mean sea level. Wild olive commonly known as Kahu (*Olea cuspidata*) is found growing in and around the drier areas of Bilaspur and Kunihar in Himachal Pradesh and in some lower parts of Jammu-Kashmir and Uttaranchal hills.

Olive tree is evergreen in nature and its botanical name is *Olea europaea* and belongs to Family *Oleaceae.* Vernacular name is Zaitun.

Trees are usually upright growing, going as high as 8 m and 6 m in spread. Trunk may be twisted and bark is of brown colour, which has splits of green colour. Canopy is almost round to oval.

Leaves are lanceolate or oblong, 2.5-7.5 cm x 3.0 cm, leathery, olive green on upper side, silvery green on the dorsal side.

Inflorescence is raceme on last year's growth. Flowers appear in panicles, are small, yellowish white and fragrant.

Fruits are fleshy drupe like that of a Jamun, having a slightly thick skin of olive green colour when half ripe that turns yellowish green on maturity. Skin is shining. Below the thick skin is fleshy layer of about 0.5 cm thickness, which is around the hard seed, that resembles the Jamun or date seed in shape, but smaller in size than these.

One fruit has only one seed and is oily.

Trees are found growing as avenue trees along the paths, ridges and in open places, as landscape trees and some planned plantations for extraction of olive oil. These are also planted as wind-breaks.

Fruits are valued for pickle and the seeds for oil content. Both have medicinal value. Olive oil is used in medicinal and cookery preparations. Wood is used for agricultural and domestic purposes.

SANDAN

Basically, it is a tree of Central India but is found as far as north in Dehradun area under the sub-Himalayan tract and outer Himalayan valleys upto an elevation of 1200 m from the River Sutlej to Sikkim. It is a tree of sub-tropical climate. It is found in mixed forests in Chamba, Kullu and like areas in Himachal Pradesh and other States.

Botanical name of the tree is *Ougeinia oojeinensis* (Roxb.) Hochreut and it belongs to Family *Fabaceae*. It is synonym to *O. dalbergioides* Benth.

It is deciduous in nature and can grow on different types of soils and under various climatic conditions so can be a large tree under congenial conditions of growth.

Leaves are shed in January-February and new leaves appear in March-April. Leaves are pinnately trifoliate, stipulate, leaflets coriaceous, unequal, the terminal largest, broad oval, the two laterals opposite oblique, edges undulate, or slightly crenate.

Flowers are lilac or white in colour, appear in racemes in February-March before the emergence of new leaves.

Pods are linear oblong, flat, 5-10 cm long, light brown and contracted between the seeds, 2-5 seeds in each pod.

Seeds are flat and have thin seed-coat.

Leaves are lopped for fodder, which is of good quality. Wood is a valuable timber. Wood is grey, durable, less liable to termite attack. Bark is used as medicine.

Phoenix Dactylifera

DATE-PALM

Trees grow best under warm and drier climate in tropical region and are also seen in sub-tropical region, but they must have sufficient moisture around their roots. Top must experience high temperature. Thus, they are found in tropical areas which are quite sunny.

Commonly known as the Date and in vernacular, it is Khajoor when fresh but dried one is known as Chhuara. Botanical name of the tree in *Phoenix dactylifera* Linn. and it belongs to Family *Araceae.*

It is an evergreen tree with a straight cylindrical stem, often going as high as 30 m. Bark is light brown and scaly. Canopy is umbrella shaped.

Leaves are pinnate, 45-50 cm long, narrow, stiff, borne in pairs, upturned, glaucous with linear acuminate segments and spiny stalk. As tree grows in height, older leaves are shed and new leaves appear on top and as such scars of stalks of fallen old leaves appear on the trunk.

Inflorescence is enclosed in a spathe on a branched spaedix, yellowish small flowers are borne singly.

Fruit is a berry with fleshy pericarp and with a deep longitudinal groove dilated inward, sweet and edible, 2.5 cm x 1.5 cm, cylindrical and brown in colour.

One seed in each fruit, which is in the centre of the pulp, light brown, 2 cm x 0.4 cm, with pointed ends, hard coated with a prominent groove.

Fruits are valued both fresh as well as dried. Leaves are used for basketry. Medicinal value of fruits and seeds is well known to users. Wood is used for domestic purposes and for long logs due to its hardy nature and water-resistance.

Fresh fruits contain 59.2 g moisture, 1.2 g protein, 0.4 g fat, 1.7 g mineral matter, 3.7 g fibre, 33.8 g carbohydrates, 22 mg calcium, 38 mg phosphorus, 0.96 g iron, 0.12 mg magnessium, 0.05 mg copper, 0.03 mg manganese, 0.03 mg zinc, 0.004 mg chromium, and Vita A 26 I.U., Thiamine 0.01 mg, Riboflavin 0.12 mg, Niacin 0.9 mg, Vita C 1.2 mg, calorific value is 144 Kcal per 100 g of edible portion.

Picea Smithiana

WESTERN HIMALAYAN SPRUCE

Trees predominantly found growing in the inner Himalayas from Afghanistan to central Nepal, are associated with specie like *Abies pindrow, Cedrus deodara, Pinus wallichiana*, etc. between 2150-3350 m elevation.

Botanical name is *Picea smithiana* (Wallich) Boiss and Family is *Conifereae* to which the conifers belong. In vernacular (Hindi) the tree is known by the name of Rai.

It is a tall tree often growing higher than 40 m or so with a conical canopy. Branches are whorled, spreading and pendulous at the ends. Bark is greyish brown and shallowly creviced into rounded or four-sliced scales.

Leaves spirally arranged, are needle like, stiff, blue or grey green, 2.5 cm to 4 cm at 60 degrees to the twigs.

Cones appear in April-May, which become pendulous on ripening and are generally dark brown and shining, 10-15 cm long with a diameter of 2.5 cm to 5 cm.

Seed 5 mm across with a cm long wing.

Timber is not of very good quality so the wood is used for making planks, boxes, shingles, pulp for paper, fuel, charcoal, etc.

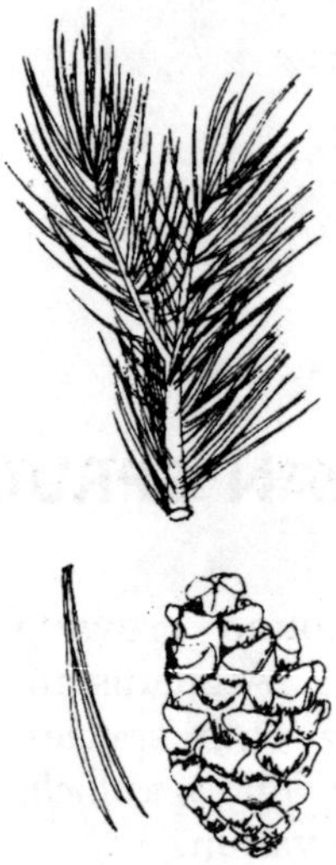
Pinus Gerardiana

CHILGOZA

Trees are found growing in parts of Himachal Pradesh, Jammu and Kashmir and Uttaranchal in dry temperate zone where there is almost no rain in the rainy season. They are found in dry valleys from 1800 m-3000 m above mean sea level, particularly in Kinnaur district of Himachal Pradesh where they are found growing as wild trees.

The tree in vernacular is known as Chilgoza or Neoza and botanical name is *Pinus gerardiana* Wallich ex Lambert belonging to Family *Pinaceae*, having many conifer trees.

Trees are evergreen almost 20 m high with a spread of 6-8 m. Canopy may be cone like to oval. Bark is dark brown in colour, which peels off in large cracks when mature to give place to new bark.

Leaves are 5 to 10 cm long, needle like, green, slightly shining, thin and smooth.

Mature cones are glaucous, 10-20 cm x 7-11 cm with very thick woody scales and stout recurved apices.

Seeds have hard seed-coat, 1.5-2.5 cm in length and 0.5 cm in diameter with one end pointed and the other round, brown.

Seeds are edible and considered a luxury dry fruit. These are eaten after roasting. The nutritive value of the seed per 100 g is as follows:

Moisture 4.0 g, protein 13.9 g, fat 49.3 g, mineral matter 2.8 g, fibre 1.0 g, carbohydrates 29.0 g, calcium 91 mg, phosphorus 49.4 mg, iron 3.6 mg, Thiamine 0.32 mg, Riboflavin 0.30 mg, Niacin 3.0 mg, Calorific value is 615 Kcal per 100 g.

Cones are used for fuel as they contain resin, which helps in their early burning.

Wood is strong, hardy and highly valuable. Trees are quite hardy to grow in stony or gravelly soil but trees are difficult to propagate.

Pinus roxburghii

CHIR PINE

Trees are found growing from 1000 m - 2000 m above mean sea level in the outer ranges and in valleys of the Himalayas and on ridges of the Shivalik flanking the Himalayas.

Botanical name of the specie is *Pinus roxburghii* Sargent and is synonym to *Pinus longifolia* Roxb. belonging to *Pinaceae* Family. In common, the trees are known as Long-leafed Pine tree but in vernacular they are known as Chil or Chir in the lower belts of their presence.

It is a coniferous tree. It is a beautiful but large evergreen tree going as high as 25 m or so under normal conditions. The spread of the tree may be 6-10 m when fully developed. Though it is an evergreen tree but may behave nearly deciduous under dry conditions. Usually on the emergence of new leaves, old leaves are shed. Trees are usually elongated in their young stage but become spreading, round or umbrella shape when mature. Bark is thick, light brown to dark brown in colour, deeply fissured and rough.

Leaves are needle-like, 20-30 cm and dark green like flower, as they appear in clusters, shining and resinous.

Cones may be solitary or in clusters, ovoid, conical and 10-15 cm x 8-13 cm.

The tree is ornamental and good as an avenue tree, which looks graceful when planted in isolation, but the trees are mostly raised as forest trees. Wood is of good quality as the heartwood is moderately hard, light, reddish brown in colour, somewhat coarse, so used for making furniture, building houses, boxes, handles of agricultural and other tools. Softwood is on the other side of the heartwood, which is whitish pink or yellow, and is used for making packing cases.

Bark yields tannin, which is used in dyeing. Oil of turpentine and resin are extracted from the tree trunk. It is used in medicines. Cones are used as fuel as they do have some resins and are easy to burn.

Trees are quite hardy and may be planted on rocky soils but no bush or other crop is generally possible under its canopy.

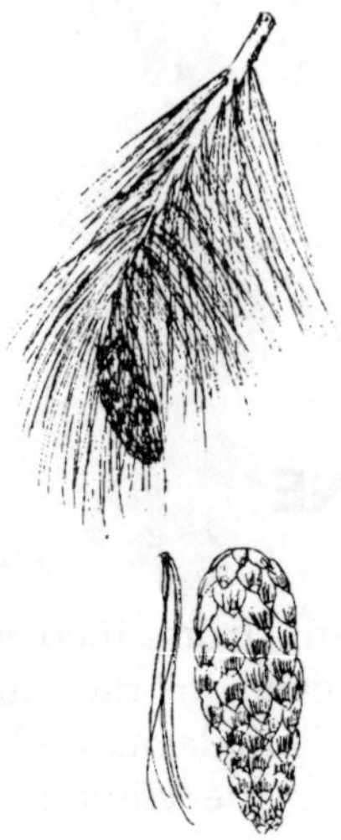

Pinus Wallichiana

HIMALAYAN BLUE PINE

As the name indicates, this pine species is found growing almost in whole of the Himalayan region right from Jammu and Kashmir to Kumaon region of Uttaranchal in the high hill regions ranging from 1800 m - 4300 m above mean sea level. It is mostly met in drier as well as wet areas as a forest tree.

Botanical name of the tree is *Pinus wallichiana* A.B. Jackson belonging to Family *Pinaceae*.

It is an evergreen symmetrical pyramidal tree going to almost 50 m in height. Bark is smooth, slate grey, which becomes rough and shallowly fissured on mature trees. Canopy is pyramidal with a spread of 6 m - 8 m.

Leaves are 15-20 cm long, needle like, shining, slender, drooping, grey, borne in short shoots in clusters of 5.

Cones are ovoid to conical in shape, green when young but turn brown on maturity, 15-25 cm long and pendulous.

Wood is highly resinous, used for local construction in carpentry, for manufacture of match boxes, tea chests and other domestic articles. Turpentine oil is received from the tree. Wood is used as fire wood. Cones are used for burning.

Platanus Orientalis

CHINAR

Though the trees of this species are of eastern Mediterranean region, but they are extensively found in Kashmir valley and other areas where they have easy access to water or humidity as they can not tolerate drought, especially during their younger stage of establishment and growth. They are found within latitudinal range of 700 m - 2700 m above mean sea level. Trees are predominantly found in Kashmir but some trees are also found in mid-hills of Himachal Pradesh and parts of Uttaranchal.

Trees are generally referred as *Platanus orientalis* Linn., which belongs to the Family *Platanaceae.* These are deciduous in nature, shedding their leaves in October. Trees are large and tall going usually upto 30 m with a spread of 5-6 m. The main trunk is mostly cylindrical and round having smooth, thin, light grey, greenish white to silver and scaling or peeling bark splits up into large but thin scales of silver grey colour.

Leaves are large, 10-15 cm across with 2-10 cm long petiole, glabrous, green, with toothed margins, palmately shaped. The petiole is generally thicker near its base to provide a protective cap to bud. Leaves are shed during autumn and new leaves appear during the spring season (late March or early April).

2-6 flowers appear at one place in April-May soon after the emergence of new leaves. Flowers are long stalked.

Fruiting head is 2-4 cm in diameter consisting of numerous 1-5 seeded achenes, densely clothed at the base with long fine hairs. They ripen in June-July.

Seeds are small, hairy and easily dispersible.

Though trees are able to grow at lower altitudes where they need irrigation but do not have good growth as they have at higher altitudes. These trees are ornamental and shady in nature.

Trees are ornamental, mostly planted along the roads, paths, borders and other such places. Wood is yellowish or reddish white, which is semi-hard and is of commercial value for making boxes, packing cases, fancy articles and domestic items. Cabinets are also made out of its wood.

Bark is used in local medicines. Fuel quality is excellent.

Plumeria Acutifolia

TEMPLE TREE

Trees are also known by the name of Chameli (in Hindi). Trees are found growing in plains and lower hills but is suitable for moist and warm places. Trees are mostly planted near roads, in parks, near temples and in isolation.

Botanical name of the species is *Plumeria acutifolia* Poir, which belongs to Family *Apocynaceae*.

Trees are deciduous in nature. They are usually large bushes or small trees with crooked but thick branches, which are cylindrical and glabrous. Bark is grey and smooth.

Leaves are 15-20 cm long and 4-6 cm broad, lanceolate, crowded at the end of branches, tapering on both ends, coriaceous, glabrous above, more or less hairy beneath, prominent but with parallel mid veins, green and with 4 cm long petiole.

Flowers are large, fragrant, white with a pale yellow centre and 4-6 cm across.

Bloom appears in March, April and then next flush is from July to October.

Fruits are two horn like pods borne on a long pendant stalk.

Seeds are with tassel of silk.

Trees are mostly multiplied by stem cuttings, which are planted during monsoon.

It is a good ornamental bush, which also serves the purpose of an avenue or roadside tree. Bark is used as a medicine, by tribals as it is purgative. Flowers are used for decoration and worship.

Plumeria Alba

WHITE FRANGIPANI

Trees are mostly found near the temples and churches. They are found growing in sub-tropical regions where frost is not very damaging but trees prefer warm and moist climate.

Another name for this tree is Pagoda Tree since its shape resembles to pagoda.

Botanical name of the tree is *Plumeria alba* Linn., which belongs to Family *Apocynaceae*.

Trees are generally deciduous in nature but may retain some leaves in coastal areas. They are 4-5 m tall with a spread of 4-5 meters. Canopy is round. Branches are few but strong at their bases and mostly grow upward with good crotch angles. Branches, particularly, the younger branches are brittle. Bark is light grey to brown and slightly scaly.

Leaves are green, 15 cm x 5 cm, ovate, hairy on dorsal side, long petioled, tapering towards apex, mid-rib prominent.

Flowers are white, showy, fragrant, waxy, appear in the spring season along with leaves. They may also appear in autumn.

Fruits are borne in pairs, long, cylindrical and are pendulous pods. They are not seen in this country.

Plants are multiplied by stem cuttings, which ooze out latex when removed from the branch. Take the semi-hard wood cuttings for propagation, let its latex dry up before planting.

Trees prefer sunny side and good soil. They are good for landscaping and avenue purposes. They also have medicinal value.

Polyalthia Longifolia

MAST TREE

Trees are mostly found growing in the Eastern and Southern parts of the country, where it flourishes well in warm and moist regions. It is also found growing wild in South India.

Botanical name of the tree is *Polyalthia longifolia* Benth and Hook f. which belongs to the family *Annonaceae*. Vernacular name is Asoka.

The trees are evergreen and handsome in nature and may go as high as 12 m with a spread of 4 to 6 m and have slender but straight branches that are usually horizontal in spread, crown is pyramidal, entirely glabrous; bark is smooth and dark greenish brown.

Leaves are lanceolate, long (10-15 cm), acuminate, margins wavy and light green in colour and shining.

Flowers are star shaped, yellowish green to scarlet red, borne on long slender stalks. They appear in early spring from February to April in umbels.

Fruits are egg shaped. They ripen in July-August.

Trees are usually raised as avenue, ornamental, landscaping or windbreak. Wood is light and flexible that is used for making pencils, boxes, drum cylinders, etc. Leaves are used for decoration of doors and gates.

Populas Ciliata

POPLAR

It is a common tree found growing from sea-coast to high hills as there are many varieties and species of this genus *Populus* available for planting under different agro-climatic conditions. This is an introduced species. Within a span of few decades, these trees have become popular throughout the country and hills are no exception. Even the hybrids are available that can adapt to various climate conditions.

Tree belongs to the Family *Salicaceae* and there are many specie like *Populus ciliata* Wall., *P. alba, P. deltoides, P. nigra,* etc., which are found growing under different conditions. They are all deciduous in nature i.e., shed their leaves during autumn or early winter.

Height of the tree is usually 12-15 m with a spread of 4-5 m. Crown is usually oval but may become oblong. Bark is usually white to silver grey in colour.

Leaves are pale greenish, petiolated, ovate-lanceolate, 7-12 cm x 5-10 cm, cordate, acute, minutely hairy along the edges.

Inflorescence is drooping raceme like catkins. Flowers may appear with leaves in early spring or so. Small catkins; male catkins 5-10 cm long while female catkins are 15 cm - 22.5 cm long.

Fruit is a capsule, ovoid and 0.5 cm across.

Seeds are small and hairy.

Trees are used for roadside plantation, wind-break and for soil conservation. Wood is used for industrial use and for plywood, packing cases, paper manufacture, commercial timber, etc. Hybrid trees grow fast. Leaves are valued as fodder.

Prosopis Juliflora

WILAYATI BABOOL

Trees are found growing in tropical and sub-tropical regions which are arid, mostly in Andhra Pradesh, Haryana, Gujarat, Karnataka, Madhya Pradesh, Chhatisgarh, Maharashtra, Punjab, Rajasthan, Tamil Nadu, Uttar Pradesh, etc.

Botanical name of the species is *Prosopis juliflora* (Swartz) D.C and belongs to Family *Mimosaceae*.

It is a semi-green to evergreen tree with zigzag staggering or pendulous canopy. It is a medium sized tree of about 10 m height with nodulated but deep roots. Bark is either grey or brownish.

Leaves are almost hairy, pinnate, 2-3 leaflets in 6-8 pairs, 2 cm - 4 cm long, obliquely oblong, mid-rib prominant, reticulate veination.

Flowers appear in February and October, white, fragrant, on 5 cm - 8 cm long peduncles, which are in group of 2-4.

Pods appear in April and January which are green in the beginning and later become of yellow colour, dehiscent, hang on the tree, constricted between two seeds, usually curved and 8 cm - 10 cm long.

Seeds are small, round to flat, hard and needs pre-sowing treatment.

Trees provide shade. Wood is used for parquet floors, construction of huts, for agricultural implements, as fence posts and cheap furniture. Leaves are used as cattle fodder while pods are used as food, powdered seeds after roasting are added to coffee. Bark is rich in tannin. Gum as adhesive is also extracted. Honeybees collect nectar to form honey from the flowers. Tolerates well to alkaline soil so good for soil reclamation.

Prunus amygdalus

ALMOND

Trees are found commonly in temperate region where rainfall is scanty during rainy season as nuts start rotting and splitting with high humidity at the time of maturity. Trees need chilling hours to the tune of 400-600 hours during winter to complete their dormancy, which they normally receive in their areas of production between 1200-2500 meters above mean sea level.

Systematic planting of these trees is found in certain pockets where they are raised either for green almonds or for drying after maturity. They are scattered all over the mid-hill region of western Himalayas particularly the outer Himalayas where nights are cool in winter and days are hot in summer and there is less rain during the maturity of fruits.

Common name in vernacular is Badam and botanical name is *Prunus amygdalus* Batsch. belonging to *Rosaceae* Family. It is a deciduous tree.

Trees are generally 8-10 m tall with spread of about 5-6 m, trunk is twisted and branches are upright and twisted. Bark is dark brown, which is usually cracked into scales. Canopy is irregular.

Foliage is sparse, olive green to lush green, lanceolate shaped leaves are 12 cm x 2-3 cm with a thick petiole of light green colour. Leaves are not very shining on the upper surface but their mid-ribs are prominent.

Flowers of white to pinkish colour appear in clusters along with leaves, which are usually of light green colour, and shining. Dioecious, blooms for a week during spring.

Fruits are green to yellowish green when half-ripe but yellowish brown on maturity. Drupe, 4 cm x 2 cm with pointed ends, hard cover underneath, which is a brownish skinned kernel, which is white to creamy white, sweet, nutty flavoured in two pieces.

Seeds are edible, their nutritive value per 100 g is—moisture 5.2 g, protein 20.8 g, fat 58.9 g, mineral matter 2.9 g, fibre 1.7 g, carbohydrates 10.5 g, calcium 230 mg, phosphorus 490 mg, iron 5.01 mg, magnesium

373 mg. Thiamine 0.24 mg, Riboflavin 0.57 mg, Niacin 4.4 mg, and Calorific value is 655 Kcal.

Kernels have medicinal value and they provide relief from swollen lever and jaundice, improves speech, increase memory and brain activity. Badam rogan is the main product, which is oil of almonds, and is used in a number of ways in commerce, cosmetic, confectionery and pharmaceuticals. Wood is slightly reddish, hard, good for furniture and provides excellent polishing.

Prunus Armeniaca

APRICOT

Moderately tall trees with spreading branches are found growing in the temperate region in the western Himalayas in the altitudinal range of 1200-2000 m above mean sea-level, both in the wild and cultivated forms. Trees yielding quality fruits are best under the altitudinal range of 1200-1500 m but above or below this altitude, their quality is affected. Trees must get sufficient chill for about 400 hours during winter when they are leafless.

Cultivated varieties of this specie are found abundantly in Jammu and Kashmir, Himachal Pradesh and Uttaranchal in the mid to slightly lower hills while in the wild form they are found in Kinnaur district of Himachal Pradesh where they are known as Chuli or Behmi while in the Uttaranchal hills, these are famous as Chulu. Their fruits are sub-acidic in taste, small in size and are used for drying, or their seeds are used for extraction of oil, which is used in many industrial units but for local people, the oil is used for domestic cooking and other purposes. Seeds are also used for raising plants which are later grafted or budded with suitable scions to have better quality fruits.

Apricots are commonly known as Khubani, Khumani, Khurbani, Khurmani, Jardaloo, etc. Trees belong to *Rosaceae* Family and botanical name is *Prunus armeniaca* L.

Trees are deciduous in nature, moderately tall (6-10) m with a spread of 4-8 m and having shabby branches which may start coming up near the base of the trunk and thus the trunk remains short. Bark is reddish brown to chocolate brown in colour and is scaly. Wood is dark brown and strong, which is used for furniture making and other domestic uses.

Leaves are simple, 6 cm x 4 cm, light green, thin, flat, ovate to round, but with sharp pointed ends.

Flowers appear during early spring in clusters of white coloured flowers (petals), which are fragrant and last for about 10 days. Leaves also emerge along with flowers.

Fruits are greenish yellow to golden yellow and even of orange colour, 3-6 cm x 3-8 cm, slightly hairy, round to oval in shape, stalk is green to brown in colour which may be 0.5 cm-1 cm long. Pulp is also of yellow to orange colour and its thickness varies from 0.5 cm-2 cm.

Seed is bold, smooth, flat to almond shaped and 1 in each fruit and covered by a hard cover of pinkish brown colour.

Fruits of the cultivated trees are sweet, juicy, aromatic, attractive with slightly acidic taste and a little fuzz or fibre near the seed. These are consumed either as fresh or when dried. The nutritive value of fruit is as follows:

Fresh 100 g pulp contains 85.3 g moisture, 1.0 g protein, 0.3 g fat, 0.7 g minerals, 1.1 g fibre, 11.6 g carbohydrates, 20 mg calcium, 25 mg phosphorus, 22 mg iron, 430 mg potassium, 0.11 mg copper, Vita A and Vita C are in traces while Vita B is 50 mg. Calorific value is 53 Kcal.

Seeds of some varieties are sweet and edible and are like those of almonds except that these are smaller in size. Wood is used for making handles of various hand tools and implements.

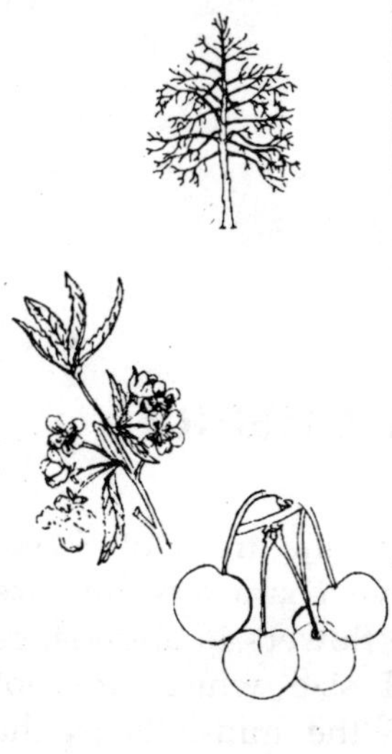

Prunus Avium

SWEET CHERRY

Trees are found in mid-hills in the upper ranges, as they need sufficient chill to complete their dormancy. Trees are not tolerant to drought for a long period. On the other hand, trees do not relish frost, but they need some moist and shady place to grow. These are planted as part of regular orchards in pockets of Himachal Pradesh, Kashmir valley and as scattered trees in mid hills of Uttaranchal within the altitudinal range of 1600-2100 m above mean sea level.

Prunus avium L. is the botanical name while its Family is *Rosaceae*. It is commonly known as cherry in English but Glas in vernacular.

Trees are deciduous in nature, almost 10- 12 m tall with a spread of 6 m or so. Canopy is oval with spreading branches. Bark is of dark brown colour when mature and is cracking in scales or fissures. Trunk is strong, liable to crack by sun if exposed for a long period. Branching is mostly upright.

Leaves appear almost along with flowers, during early spring. Leaves are green, glossy on upper surface with prominent veins, size varies between 7-12 cm x 5-7 cm. Petiole is round, light green and large of 3-4 cm length.

Flowers appear in clusters of 3-5 during the spring season, pinkish white in colour, very attractive and sweet scented, and lasts for 10 days or so.

Fruits are small, round, 1-2 cm x 1-2 cm, red, yellow, dark purple or pink in colour, sweet and pulpy. Skin is soft, smooth, shining, and edible along with pulp. Fruit stalk is usually green but may be slightly brownish, 3-5 cm in length.

Single and round to oval seed is in each fruit. Seed is hard-coated, light brown in colour 0.5 cm x 0.3 cm in size.

Fruits are used as desset fruits. Nutritive value per 100 g of fruit is—moisture 83.4 g, protein 1.1 g, fat 0.5 g, mineral matter 0.8 g, carbohydrates 12.3 g, fibre 0.9 g, calcium 10 mg, phosphorus 67 mg, iron 2 mg, Thiamine 0.02 mg, Niacin 0.6 mg, Riboflavin 0.03 mg, and Vita C 16 mg. Calorific value is 64 Kcal.

Wood is of prime quality, which is good for furniture making as it is hard and of pink to reddish brown in colour. Fruits can be dried or processed in sugar. They are also used for the dressing of the ice creams and cakes.

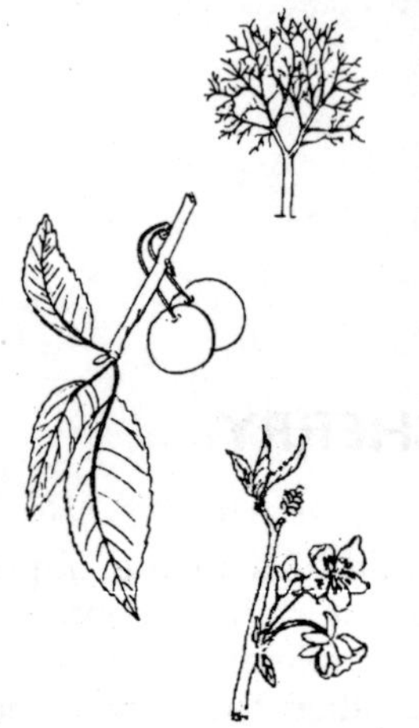

Prunus Cerasus

FLOWERING CHERRY

These trees resemble the trees of Sweet Cherry in many vegetative characters but are small in size and produce flowers in abundance and bear fruits of small size which are not edible. Trees are seen in the mid-hills in the temperate zone in all the hills of western Himalayas and they are usually between 1200 m - 2000 m above mean sea level. Trees are found on roadsides, paths, and borders and in isolation in lawns and pastures as a landscape tree. These are ornamental in nature and are shady.

Botanical name is *Prunus cerasus* Linn. and tree belongs to *Rosoceae* Family. These are deciduous in nature, leaves drop during autumn or soon after the harvest of the fruit and new leaves appear in early spring. Trees are generally 5-6 m tall and of 4 m spread but when congenial conditions are available they may be 8-10 m tall and 6-8 m in spread. Canopy is round to oval with a well-developed trunk that has a pinkish brown bark, which may be splitting or cracking.

Leaves appear along with flowers or slightly later than flowers. They are green but nearing maturity may become dirty green. 7-10 cm x 3-5 cm with pointed tips, lanceolate and with a green petiole of 2 cm length.

Flowers appear in clusters of 3-5, whitish-pink in the beginning but loose their pink colour soon at full bloom. Bloom lasts for a fortnight or so. These trees flower first of all the specie of the temperate trees in the season.

Fruits are small, 0.5 cm x 0.5 cm, round, brown to purplish red in colour, pulp is almost negligible and remains with the seed.

Seed is one in each fruit, light brown smooth and 0.3 cm x 0.3 cm.

Trees are ornamental in nature. Wood is used for making furniture and other domestic articles. Good for honeybees and for development and improvement of marginal lands. Seeds and fruits are not edible.

Prunus Domestica

PLUM

Commonly known as Alubakhara or Alucha trees are found growing in orchards. These are cultivated fruit trees, which are found in many parts of Himachal Pradesh, Jammu and Kashmir, Uttaranchal and adjoining areas in the altitudinal range between 1000-1600 m above mean sea level, mostly in the mid-hills and valleys.

Trees grow best when nights are cool and they need chill for about 400-600 hours or so during winter when the temperature should be 7°C or below. Dry spell at the time of flowering and fruit development is quite damaging to the growth of the tree and its yield. This causes small fruits, which may drop: on the other hand, high humidity causes splitting of ripe fruits.

There are two species found growing: common plum is *Prunus salicina* known as Japanese plum or prune while European plum is *Prunus domestica* L. and both belong to *Rosaceae* Family. Most of the characters of both types are identical except the shape of fruits. Trees are deciduous in nature and may go as high as 10 m but usually they remain 5-6 m tall with spread of even diameter. Bark is scaly, brown and splitting. Branches are usually upright in the earlier stage but droop on maturity. Canopy is round to oval with enough green foliage during summers.

Leaves are elliptical with serrated margins, thin, dark green on the upper side while light green on the lower side, 6-10 cm x 3-5 cm, petoiled and shining.

Flowers appear during spring, almost along with the leaves, white, in clusters and many in numbers. Trees look beautiful during bloom, which may last for 7-10 days. Size of flowers is small about 0.75 cm-1 cm.

Fruits are oval or egg shaped, fleshy, juicy, variable in size from 3-5 cm x 4-6 cm with a round stalk of 1 cm length, and of light brown colour. The colour of skin may be yellow, golden, green or purple while the pulp may be yellow to red in colour, which is sweet, juicy and slightly fragrant. In most varieties, the skin is sweet but in some cases, it is slightly sour and thicker.

One seed is in the centre of fruit, cling or non-cling, light to dark brown in colour, round to oblong, 1 cm-1.5 cm, hard and pointed on one end.

Fruits when mature are used as dessert fruits but they do not remain good and fit for use for more than a week after harvest. Fruits are of various shapes, colours and sizes depending upon the variety. Pulp can be used for making jam, jelly, nectar, etc. They can also be dried and used at later stages. Oil is extracted from the kernels of seeds. Wood is good for furniture making and other uses. Wood is of dark brown colour and hard.

Nutritive value of mature fruits is—100 g pulp contains moisture 86.9 g, fat 0.5 g, protein 0.7 g, mineral matter 0.4 g, fibre 0.4 g, carbohydrates 11.1 g, calcium 10 mg, phosphorus 12 mg, iron 2.42 mg, magnesium 147 mg, potassium 247 mg, iron 2.42 mg, sulphur 33 mg, Vita A 230 I.U., Thiamine 120 mg, Riboflavin 30 mg, Niacin 0.30 mg and Vita C 1 mg. Calorific value is 52 Kcal.

BIRD CHERRY

This species is found growing in the hills of Himalayas often in the altitudinal range between 2000-3000 m above mean sea level, right from Pakistan (Koh-murree) to Sikkim through Jammu and Kashmir, Himachal Pradesh and Uttaranchal. Trees are seen scattered on ridges, near paths and in grasslands.

This belongs to the Family *Rosaceae* and the botanical name is *Prunus padus* Linn.

Trees are deciduous in nature. Bark is slightly fissured and light brown in colour.

Height of the tree is almost 6-8 m with a spread of 4-6 m under normal conditions as these are not cared for. Crown is oval to oblong and bark colour is brown to dark bark brown with sputs.

Leaves are shed during winter and new leaves appear in spring along with flowers.

Leaves are green, ovate or ovate-lanceolate, 10-15 cm, minutely toothed, long, pointed, stipules linear, soon falling off.

Flowers appear in clusters, 1 cm in diameter, white in colour, in drooping racemes, which are 7-10 cm long.

Fruit is globose, red turning to dark purple or black and acidic, which ripens in June-July.

Trees are ornamental in nature and are found along paths, etc. Wood is of medium quality.

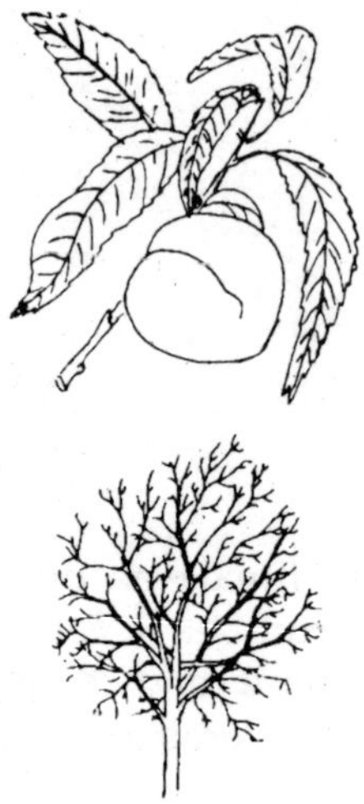

Prunus Persica

PEACH

Commonly it is known as Aaroo in almost all the hilly areas along the Himalayan belt. Well planned orchards of peach trees are found in the mid-hill and lower hills of western Himalayas in all the belts right from Jammu and Kashmir to North East India. Though some varieties are available which grow under lower elevations but their quality is not good due to non-fulfilment of their dormancy requirement. Good quality and sweet juicy fruits are available under mid-hill areas.

Garhwal and Kumaon regions of Uttaranchal; Solan, lower areas of Shimla, Sirmaur, Kullu, Chamba and parts of Mandi district of Himachal Pradesh and lower parts of Kashmir valley and upper areas of Jammu have these trees where they get chill for 300-500 hours during which the temperature remains around 7°C during winter. Best growth is between 1000 m-1300 m above mean sea level.

Botanical name of the tree is *Prunus persica* (Linn.) Batsch which belongs to Family *Rosaceae*. In Hindi, it is known as Aroo. It is a deciduous tree, mostly 6-8 m tall and of even spread with round to oval canopy, which is usually asymmetrical. Trunk is short but stout with weak angled branches that yield spreading branches. Bark is dark brown and scaly, which splits off easily.

Leaves are green, leathery, glossy and smooth on upper side but slightly hairy or rough on their lower sides, lanceolate, saw-toothed or wavy margins, 15 cm x 6 cm, petiole is light green and round. Young leaves are pinkish green and narrow.

Flowers are axillary; pink and many appearing before the emergence of leaves and bloom lasts for 7-10 days. Bloom provides attractive look to the trees.

Fruits are round to oval, slightly hairy, greenish-yellow with a pink blush. Flesh is cream to yellowish pink, sweet, juicy, skin tight but edible, 5-8 cm x 4-8 cm, thickness of flesh ranges from 1-2 cm.

Seed one, in centre of pulp, which may be cling or non-cling, hard coated, deep pitted stone with elaborate pattern of ridges and hollows, light brown to pinkish brown and 1.5 cm x 1 cm.

Trees are mostly raised for their fruits which are sweet and juicy. Pulp may be separable or unseparable from the seed. Fruits are highly perishable when mature. Unripe and over ripe fruits are of no use for commerce as they either shrivel or become flaccid and lose their turgidity. Nearly mature fruits are canned in sugar syrup as halves. They can also be processed to make jam, squash, nectar and other drinks. Fruits are eaten when fresh. Wood is brown and good for making handles of agricultural implements and hand-tools.

Fruits are eaten fresh when almost full mature. Their nutritive value per 100 g is—moisture 86.0 g, protein 1.3 g, fat 0.3 g, mineral matter 0.8 g, fibre 1.2 g, carbohydrates 10.5 g, Vita C 3 mg, Vita A 150 I.U., Vita B 30 mg, calcium 8 mg, phosphorus 15 mg, and iron 0.5 mg, Calorific value is 50 Kcal.

PAJA

Trees are found growing here and there is pastures, grasslands and community lands in the mid-hills of the Himalayan belt right from Pakistan to Bhutan and even upto Arunachal Pradesh. Usually, the range of altitudinal variation is from 1000 m to 2000 m above mean sea level.

Botanical name if the species is *Prunus puddum* Roxb. and this belongs to Family *Rosaceae.*

It is also known as Painyan in Garhwal and Kumaon region of Uttaranchal.

Trees are deciduous in nature.

Trees are not very large and often 5-6 m tall with an even spread. Canopy is round to oval with good foliage and spreading branches. Main trunk remains small but stout. Bark is of pink to greyish pink in colour, which does not split soon.

Leaves ovate, 7 to 10 cm long and 3-5 cm wide, pointed at the tips, stalks glandular, stipules long, 3-5 parted, green and shining on upper surfacc.

Flowers are of pink colour, many, solitary or in small clusters and crowded towards the end of branches. They appear in early winter when other temperate trees are leafless.

Fruits are ovoid, red or yellow, drupe and acidic.

Seed is usually wrinkled or furrowed and ovoid.

Bud-sticks of trees are used as rootstock for Sweet Cherry. Wood is of medium to good quality and is used for making of handles of agricultural hand tools, other small boxes, etc.

Psidium Guajava

GUAVA

It is a common man's apple as its nutritive value is almost equal to apple and is grown abundantly throughout the country where its yield per tree and total production is much more than apple. Since the trees are susceptible to spring frost, they have limited pockets of their occurrence in the hills and valleys. On the other hand, mature trees are quite hardy and resistant to both drought and frost. They need protection from frost and drought during their early stage of growth.

Since the trees can grow on marginal lands, which may be coarse, less fertile and shallow, they are raised even in grasslands and on slopes. Guava generally known as Amrood in vernacular, belongs to the Family *Myrtaceae* and the botanical name is *Psidium guajava* Linn. which is evergreen in nature and may behave deciduous in hills.

Trees are 6-8 m tall with an equal spread; oblong to round in shape with smooth bark of pink colour, which is papery and peels off readily. Branching is strong and upright with spreading habit.

Foliage is sparse, leaves are light green in colour, leathery, swollen, oval to oblong in shape, and opposite, petioled, 6-8 cm x 3-5 cm, pointed towards their free ends.

Flowers are small and of white colour, which appear in spring. They may appear twice in a year in some cases.

Fruits are round to oval in shape, cream to yellow with red blush on the skin while the pulp is cream or pinkish in colour, which is sweet and aromatic, size is 5-10 cm x 5-10 cm. Flesh or pulp along with skin and seeds are edible.

Seeds are small, pinkish brown and hard when mature.

Guava trees are valued for their fruits, which have nutritive and medicinal value. The nutritive value per 100 g is—moisture 53.0 g, protein 0.1 g, fat 0.2 g, mineral matter 0.6 g, fibre 4.8 g, carbohydrates 9.0 g, calcium 50 mg, phosphorus 20 mg, iron 1-2 mg, magnesium 24 mg, potassium 91 mg, sulphur 14 mg. Thiamine 30 mg, Niacin 0.2 mg, Riboflavin 30 mg and ascorbic acid 299 mg, Calorific value is 38-66 Kcal.

Fruits are used for dessert purposes and, they can be processed into jam, jelly, nectar, candy, etc. Fruits are laxative in nature and used against a number of diseases. Wood is used for making handles of various hand-tools and for domestic use.

INDIAN KINO

It is widely distributed tree throughout the greater part of the Indian Peninsula in deciduous forests and to limited extent in Sub-Himalayan tracts from Haldwani in Uttaranchal and eastward to Gorakhpur in Uttar Pradesh. It is quite common in Madhya Pradesh, Chhatisgarh, Gujarat, Maharashtra, Andhra Pradesh, Orissa, Karnataka, Kerala and Tamil Nadu.

Bijasal or Bijsar is botanically known as *Pterocarpus marsupium* Kurz, which belongs to Family *Papilionaceae*.

Trees are deciduous in nature. They are tall with spreading branches forming a round canopy, branches are hairy.

Leaves are compound having 7-9 leaflets and are 8-13 cm long, oval-oblong, mucronate, silky but hairy beneath. Petioles are hairy.

Flowers are yellow, 1.5 cm long, scented in simple tawny pubescent axillary racemes, bloom in April-May-June.

Fruit is 2.5 cm long, round, velvety and hairy but winged with one seed.

Ripe pods are collected in February, dried and stored in gunny bags. Plants are raised by seeds which are sown in the spring season and later transplanted during the monsoon season.

Timber received from the tree is valued for structural use as it is durable. Leaves are used as fodder. Wood and bark are used in medicines for diabetes. Leaves, flowers and gum of the tree are of medicinal use.

Punica Granatum

POMEGRANATE

Though trees relish dry period during monsoon, cool during winter but warm during summer and enough fertile soil for their best growth but they are also found growing in lower to mid-hills of the Himalayas where they are as large bushes or small trees. They are found growing along the road-sides, on marginal lands and wastelands or even in pastures. In plains, there are planned orchards. The altitudinal range for good growth of trees and production is from 400-1200 m above mean sea level. Since the trees are grown mainly for their fruits, they do not need rain during the time of their maturity but under the Himalayan conditions, mostly there are rains during the period of maturity of fruit, which is the rainy season. So they remain of small size, thick skinned, less pulpy and crack open.

Botanical name of the tree is *Punica granatum* Linn. and it belongs to the family *Punicaceae*. Local name is Anar or Daru. It is an evergreen, fast growing, weak stemmed tree growing more like a bush under hill conditions on rocky slopes.

Branching is generally upright, which becomes spreading during fruiting. Bark is light brown and may have fissures.

Leaves are lush green, oblong, glossy with short petioles, opposite, 5-7 cm x 2 cm.

Flowers are of deep red colour, which are due to colour of the petals that look attractive under the background of lush green leaves. They appear during summer and are moderately medium in size but conspicuous from a distance.

Fruits are oval or globe shaped, yellow to bright red in colour, 6 cm-10 cm in diameter. Skin is thick, sometimes glossy and leathery. Inside many loculii, each containing many seeds enclosed by a rich pulp of yellow to red colour. Sweet and slightly acidic in taste. Seeds and pulp both are edible. In case of small fruits, which are almost of wild nature, the fruits are acidic with small seeds and less pulp.

Under normal conditions the nutritive value per 100 g of edible portion is: moisture 78.0 g, protein 1.6 g, fat 0.1 g, carbohydrates 14.5 g, calcium 10 mg, phosphorus 70 mg, iron 1.7 mg, magnesium 44 mg, potassium 133 mg, sulphur 12 mg, Thiamine 20 mg, Riboflavin 100 mg, Niacin 30 mg, mineral matter 0.7 g, fibre 5.1 g, ascorbic acid 16 mg, and Calorific value is 65 Kcal.

Roots, bark and seeds are of medicinal value particularly to improve digestion. Refreshing drink prepared out of juice of pulp and seed provides relief from the warm weather. Anardana, dried seeds along with pulp is used in a number of domestic preparations in various dishes. Fruits are relished as a dessert.

Pyrus Communis

PEAR

Pear trees are so diversified in their agro-climatic requirements that they are found in almost all types of climates and on all types of soils. Best quality fruits are obtained in the temperate region of western Himalayas where they have thin skin, sweet juice and creamy flesh. Quality pears are available from Kashmir.

Most of the trees are found growing as seedling trees in all areas in the Himalayan region ranging between 920-2700 m above mean sea level. They are mostly scattered along roadsides, on boundaries, wastelands and marginal lands. In some places pear scions have been grafted over Kainth. (*Pyrus pashia).*

Pear is also known as Nakh, Nashpati, Babugosha, etc. Its botonical name is *Pyrus communis* Linn. and it belongs to family *Rosaceae.* It is deciduous in nature and may be 10-15 m in height and about 5-8 m in spread. Canopy is usually oblong to conical but it may be round. Trunk is usually straight, stout, with blackish brown bark, which is generally cracked to form scales. Branching is upright and then going slightly horizontal.

Leaves are oval, 15 cm x 5 cm, green to brownish green in colour, toothed at margins, glossy and pointed towards the tip, lower surface is slightly rough and less green than the upper side, Veins quite prominent but not the network.

Flowers are of white colour, which appear during spring season in clusters, along with leaves.

Fruits are typically pear shaped, oblong to round with green to yellowish pink skin on maturity. The skin may be soft or hard, with or without lenticels but is edible. Flesh greenish white to cream in colour, slightly scented, sweet, juicy. Size is 7-10 cm x 5-10 cm with a strong but round stalk of 3-5 cm length, which is light brown in colour that remains with the fruit even after maturity.

5-10 seeds are placed in the core of fruit. They are round on one end while the other end is pointed, dark brown, glossy, hard, 0.5 cm x 0.3 x 0.1 cm.

Fruits are edible, half-ripe fruits are used for cooking as a vegetable and pickling; full sized mature fruits are used for making jam and preserves. Wood is used for making furniture and agricultural tools and for various domestic purposes.

Nutritive value of fruit per 100 g is—moisture 86.0 g, protein 0.6 g, fat 0.2 g, minerals 0.3 g, fibre 1.0 g, carbohydrates 11.9 g, calcium 8 mg, phosphorus 15 mg, iron 0.5 mg, Vita A 28 I.U., Thiamine 0.06 mg, Riboflavin 0.03 mg, Niacin 0.2 mg, Vita C in traces and energy released is 52 Kcal.

Pyrus Pashia

KAINTH

These trees are found growing in whole of Himalayan and Shivalik ranges in wild state and are used for grafting of good scions to get the pear fruits of commerce. They are mostly found in the range of 750-2700 m above mean sea level under varied soil conditions on marginal lands and pastures. They span from Himachal Pradesh to Kumaon hills in Uttaranchal under Himalayan belt.

Botanically the tree is known as *Pyrus pashia* Buch. Ham. which belongs to *Rosaceae* Family.

It is generally a medium sized tree, which is usually 6-8 m tall with spread of 4-6 m. Trunk is stout with profuse branching. Bark is dark brown and scaly, which splits in mature trees. Canopy is oval in general.

Leaves are ovate to broadly lanceolate, long, pointed, toothed, glossy on upper surface but hairless, shining when mature, 5-10 cm, young leaves are woolly.

Flowers appear in clusters along with leaves during spring season, white, 2-2.5 cm across, petals obovate with darker veins, Dioecious.

Fruits are globular pome, 1.3-2.5 cm, dark brown with raised lenticels.

Seeds are small, dark brown and many in a single fruit.

Fruits are edible but not liked by all.

Leaves are used for cattle fodder. Wood is bit hard, reddish brown, compact, fine grained and durable, which is used for manufacture of small implements, handles of hand tools and for fuel purposes.

Quercus Dilatata

TILONJ

Trees are found growing in Western Himalayas spanning from North-Western Himalaya to Afghanistan in Jammu-Kashmir, Himachal Pradesh and Uttaranchal hills between elevations of 1800-2700 m, along the water streams in mixed forests in damp situations. It is a tree of temperate climate, which can tolerate minimum temperature of minus 6°C.

Botanical name of this tree is *Quercus dilatata* Lindley and it belongs to Family *Fagaceae*. Another vernacular name for this tree is Moor or Moru.

It is an evergreen tree having the characteristics of a common oak tree. It is a large tree with straight bole and dense crown. The bark of young trees is smooth but that of old ones is dark grey or blackish with vertical and horizontal cracks, exfoliating in rectangular or irregular scales or strips.

Leaves are leathery, lanceolate to elliptical with spiny or entire margins. Leaves are hairless from beneath. New leaves appear in April and May and simultaneously older leaves are shed.

Male catkins and female spikes appear on the new shoots in March-April and they get pollinated in 10-15 days and then start maturing.

Fruits are acorns or nuts, which are ovoid with a fine point, 1 cm in diameter, smooth, brown or greenish brown in colour, glabrous and shining. They mature in 15-17 months after pollination.

Wood of the tree is quite strong, which is used for many household and other purposes. Leaves are lopped for fodder. Kernels contain 9-31 per cent of crude protein hence are used as cattle feed supplement.

Quercus Glauca

PHANIYAT

Trees grow scattered in the valleys of outer Himalayas between altitudes of 800 m to 3000 m in moist forests, along the ravines. It is predominantly common in Kangra valley of Himachal Pradesh. Garhwal region of Uttaranchal and mid-hills of Kashmir valley.

Botanical name of the tree is *Quercus glauca* Thumb, belonging to Family *Fagaceae*. It is a large, handsome evergreen tree with a rounded crown and a clean cylindrical bole, which may not be very long.

Bark of the tree is thin, grey, smooth to rough and fissured.

Leaves oblong to oblong-lanceolate, pointed, 8-15 cm long saw-toothed, leathery and shining above. Old leaves start yellowing with the appearance of new leaves during spring (April).

Male catkins appear in March-April along with new leaves. Female flowers also appear after a fortnight of male flowers.

Fruit formation takes place soon after pollination in April-May. They attain optimum size by September but remain green. They ripe after a year in October-November.

Ripe nuts are ovoid or conical, brown, 1.5 cm to 2.5 cm long and 0.75 cm to 1.00 cm in diameter, smooth, shining and glabrous.

Wood is not of very good quality and hence used for petty purposes. Leaves provide fodder of medium quality, which are lopped in northwest Himalayas.

Quercus incana

BAN OAK

Trees are found growing from Pakistan to Central Nepal and Myanmar under the altitudinal range of 1200 to 2400 m above mean sea level, often in association with *Rhododendron arboreum* and *Lyonia ovalifolia.* It grows best on dry, grassy hillsides and adjoining areas.

Botonical name is *Quercus incana* Roxb., Syn. *Quercus leucotrichophora* A. Camus which belongs to family *Fagaceae.*

Trees are evergreen, medium to large sized, often 10-12 m with an uneven spread of 6 m or so. Branching is upright but spreading. Bark is greyish brown, cracked and exfoliating in irregular scales. Young shoots have white hairs. Canopy is oval to round.

Leaves have dense white-woolly hairs beneath, leathery, dark green, sharply toothed towards tip, 6-16 cm × 4-6 cm, stalked, ovate-lanceolate.

Acorn single or in pairs.

Nuts ovoid, 1-1.5 cm long, half encircled by the involucral cup when mature, with involucral bracts as broad as long, rough hoary, white tomentose when young but later glabrous brown.

Wood is not of very good quality so is used for domestic purposes for building construction and fuel purposes. Leaves are fed to cattle. Acorns have medicinal value. Trees are good for wasteland and marginal land.

Quercus Lanata

RIANJ

Trees of this species are found in patches in Garhwal and Kumaon areas of Uttaranchal, Arunachal Pradesh, etc. between 1800 to 2400 m elevation in forests as gregarious trees.

Botanical name is *Quercus lanata* Smith and belongs to the Family *Fagaceae*.

It is an evergreen tree, medium to large sized with a massive root system. Young shoots are with red coloured hairs.

Leaves are dark, shiny green above and contrasting rust coloured and woolly haired beneath, leathery, and elliptical to lanceolate, conspicuously toothed with 9-14 pairs of lateral veins and 8-15 cm long.

Male catkins have woolly hairs and appear in April-May.

Fruit is either solitary or in pairs, stalkless, axillary, oblong, 1.5 cm across, nut, half encircled in the woody involucral cup.

Wood is used for fuel while foliage provides fodder of good quality.

Quercus Semecarpifolia

KHARSU OAK

It is a tree of moist temperate forests in the Himalayas from Bhutan westwards; between 2400-3800 m above mean sea level. It is quite common in Western Himalayas in association with oak and fir forests. It is distinguished from other trees by rusty-brown foliage.

Botanical name of the tree is *Quercus semecarpifolia* Smith which belongs to Family *Fagaceae*. Also known by the names Moru and Khor.

It is a large evergreen tree with a spreading crown and a clean bole. Bark is dark grey, rough and with irregular scales.

Leaves are elliptical to oblong, 5-10 cm x 4-6 cm, usually with spiny marginal teeth on young trees but often with entire margins on old trees, dark green, tomentose and glossy beneath. Flush of leaves appears from April to June at lower elevations.

Flowers appear in May-June in upper area. Male catkins are 5-8 cm long, drooping and clustered while female spikes are erect and short which appear simultaneously and on the same tree.

Fruits are known as nuts or acorns, cup covering only base of the nut, which is globular, solitary, 2.5 cm across and dark brown or black when ripe. They ripen in July-August, 15 months after flowering.

Wood is used in construction work of houses, and as a good fuel. Bark contains tannin. Foliage is used as fodder.

Rhododendron Arboreum

RHODODENDRON

Number of specie of the genus *Rhododendron* are found growing from sea-coast to high altitudes but under north-western Himalayan region, the species *Rhododendron arboreum* Smith is predominantly seen on wide range of altitudes. Also known as Bras and Burans. It belongs to Family *Ericaceae*. Trees are mostly found in the range of 1500-1800 m above mean sea level on slopes on the mid hill zones of the temperate region.

Generally, trees are 10-15 m tall with a spread of about 6-7 m but they can be more taller and spreading depending upon the conditions of growth. Canopy is usually round but may become haphazard since the branches, particularly, the younger ones are brittle which on breaking or drop provide the canopy some unsystematic shape. Bark is reddish brown, which is generally cracked here and there.

Main trunk is strong with good crotch angles. Young branches break due to weight of snow during winter and plucking of flowers during spring season.

Leaves are deep green on upper surface while light green and hairy on the dorsal side, 15 cm x 5 cm in size with well marked veins, margins are serrated and the tip is somewhat pointed.

Flowers appear in bunches on terminals of shoots in the early spring. They are showy, large and remain on the tree for a week after full bloom. The petals are of red colour which are leathery. Stamens are of white colour which beautifully match contrasting to red.

Fruit is a capsule, 3 cm, ribbed, cochambered, brown in colour.

It is a national flower of Nepal. Trees are ornamental in nature, evergreen and gorgeous to look at. Flowers have medicinal value and they provide a refreshing drink when used after making squash out of them. Anthers must be separated from the flowers while extracting their juice, only the red petals should be used. Jam, jelly, chutney, etc., can be made from the flowers. Young leaves may be slightly poisonous. Wood of the tree is used for coal making, timber and fuel purposes.

Robinia Pseudo-acacia

ROBINIA

Tree is found in the humid areas of tropical region. It is successfully growing in the temperate areas of North-West Himalayas spanning from Jammu-Kashmir, Himachal Pradesh, Uttaranchal to Assam and North-Eastern States in the altitudinal range up to 2400 m above mean sea level. Best growth is between 1500 to 2000 m elevations.

Trees belong to the family *Papilionaceae* and botanical name is *Robinia pseudo-acacia* Linn. It is also famous by the name of False Acacia or Black Locust Tree.

Trees are deciduous in nature, height may be 20-25 m, trunk is erect, often bifurcated, with scaly prickly branches. Young shoots are smooth, purplish brown, with triangular spines in pairs, which remain for some years. Bark is deeply longitudinally fissured and of grey brownish colour.

Leaves are pale-green to blue green, alternate, pinnate, composed of 7-20 leaflets, have two strong thorns, which become stipules at the base of stalk.

Inflorescence is pendulous raceme. Flowers are white, fragrant, sweet scented, appear in clusters in April-May and are 2 cm across.

Fruits are pendulous pods, leathery, red brown when ripe and have 4-10 kidney shaped seeds. They mature in September-October.

Seeds are wax-coated, hard and impervious to water.

It is a multipurpose tree, which is used as an avenue, shady, roadside plantation and flowering tree and for lopping fodder. Best suited for conservation of unstable land and ground. Timber quality is good. Honeybees suck the sap from the flowers. Poles are also made from the tree. Wood is decay resistant and hardy. Bark is poisonous.

Salix Alba

WHITE WILLOW

These are not of ancient origin but are the introduced trees which are mostly planted along water coarses or in moist places. Mostly they are found growing in the temperate region but here these are growing in moist areas under sub-tropical region. It is known as White Willow due to colour of leaves which are silky and canes are also almost white.

This has the botanical name, *Salix alba* Linn which belongs to the family *Salicaceae.* Local name is Beuns

Trees are deciduous in nature. These are not very large trees but are of medium height about 10 m tall with a trunk diameter of 60 cm. Crown is spreading composed of long rising branches. Bark is grey which cracks with age.

Leaves narrowly lanceolate, 5-10 cm, long pointed, minutely toothed, white silky on both surfaces when young, the upper becoming glabrous when old.

Flowers appear during spring, particularly, in April after the leaves have emerged. Catkins terminating short, lateral leafy shoots, drooping : male katkins are 2-4 cm long white female catkins are 5-7 cm.

Fruits are ovoid-conic capsules which are nearly sessile and pubescent.

Seeds have white pappus, minute, yellow and ovoid.

Trees are of landscape value as they provide an attractive look to the lawn or the site. Canes or the twigs are used for making baskets and other articles of domestic use, which are long lasting and of decorative value.

Sapindus Mukorossi

SOAP NUT

Soap nut trees are found both as cultivated and wild along the Sutlej valley in the Himalayan tract ascending upto 1800 m above mean sea level.

Botanical name of the tree is *Sapindus detergens* Roxb. with syn. *S. mukorossi* Gaertn and it belongs to Family *Sapindaceae.* These are commonly known as Reetha trees since the seeds of the trees are round and hard.

Trees are deciduous in nature and are large in size, about 15 m to 18 m tall with a spread of 6-8 m. Bole is clean. Canopy is oval and spreading. Bark is of light brown to dark grey in colour. Branching is upright and then spreading horizontally.

Leaves are alternate, lanceolate, 10-15 cm long and 3 cm wide, the terminal pair is smaller, hairy leaflets 8-15, entire.

Flowers are mostly bisexual, many, small, generally 3 flowered cymes arranged in a terminal compound pyramidal thyrsus, purple, bloom in May-June.

Fruit is a fleshy drupe when young but on maturity its pulp dries up, smooth, globose, yellow 1.5 to 2.0 cm in diameter, brown on ripening.

Seed one in each fruit, round, black, 1 cm across, oily and hard.

Trees are ornamental and shady, good for roadside plantation. Pulp of the fruit is of commercial value as is used in a number of toiletry preparations and for decoration. Powder of dried pulp is used in a number of ways by local people, usually for washing clothes and preparing shampoos. Wood is used for making handles of hand-tools.

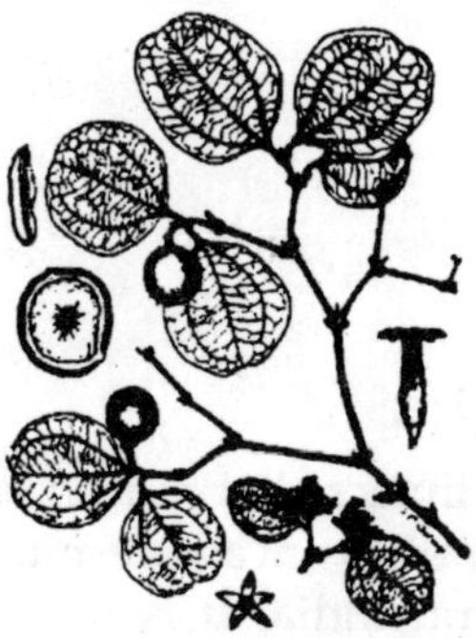

Strychnos nux-vomica

NUX-VOMICA

This is a tree of tropical region but is also found near the coastal areas in the southern and western coasts of the country and thus is also sub-tropical to large extent. It is a native tree of Malabar region of India.

Botanical name of the tree is *Strychnos nux-vomica* Linn. which belongs to the family Loganiaceae and the Hindi name is Kuchla.

Trees are evergreen and may go as high as 15 m but they are generally between 10 to 12 m. Main trunk is strong and there are many branches, which mostly grow upward. Bark is smooth and greyish.

Leaves are green, opposite, short petioled, oval and acuminate with 5 strong veins prominent on the dorsal side that is darker than the upper side.

Flowers are small, greenish white, growing in apical corymbose, bloom in early spring.

Fruits are large, equal to the size of an orange, globose, berry, and green turning reddish yellow on ripening. The flesh is white, sticky and bitter.

Seeds are 5 to 8 in each fruit, large and compressed like a button, nearly circular, flat, grey, shining and poisonous containing alkaloids.

Trees are mostly raised for the medicinal value as they are good source of strychnine and nux-vomica. Bark is used for extraction of tonic while seeds are used for extraction of various alkaloids that are used in treatment of various human and animal diseases and disorders. Wood is used for agricultural tools.

ASH

It is a small tree found growing from Himachal Pradesh to Arunachal Pradesh at altitude ranging from 2000 to 4000 m above mean sea level in western temperate Himalayas and Central India. It is mostly found in alpine forests.

Botanical name is *Sorbus foliolosa* (Wall) Spach and belongs to Family *Rosaceae*.

Trees are deciduous in nature. They may be 4-5 m in height with an equal spread. Bark peels off in horizontal strips. Twigs are nearly hairless.

Leaves are 6-12 cm long with 9-15 pairs of linear, oblong, sharp toothed, blunt or acute leaflets, which are 2.3-4 cm long.

Inflorescence is usually with white downy hairs. Flowers appear in April to June and are white or greenish white in dense flat-topped cluster, smelling unpleasantly.

Fruits are ovoid or globular in shape, red or bluish red in colour.

In West Bengal, leaves are lopped for fodder and the fodder is of medium quality.

Syzygium Cumini

JAMUN

These trees are generally found growing in association with mango trees under the identical agro-climatic conditions. These are mostly found growing below an altitude of 1000 m above mean sea level in tropical and sub-tropical regions. In the hilly areas, these are found in the lower belts of Himachal Pradesh and Uttaranchal where they get mild climate which is frost-free. They are almost grown in all the areas. Trees can tolerate frost and drought to great extent than the mango trees. Trees are seen near the paths, roads and watercourses or in grasslands.

Botanical name is *Syzygium cumini* (Linn.) Skeels Syn. *Eugenia jambolana,* Linn. and this belongs to the Family *Myrtaceae.*

Trees are evergreen in nature with large dense foliage. Trees are quite tall up to 10 m with a spread of 5-6 m. Canopy is oval to round. Bark is grey brown, smooth with slight depressions. Branching is strong.

Young leaves which are coppery appear during spring while older leaves are green, shining and bit leathery in texture with a round petiole of 1-1.5 cm length, elliptical with a tip, 10 cm x 3-5 cm in size, veins are prominent on the dorsal side.

In late winter, flowers of greenish colour appear in clusters, which are sweet scented and small in size.

Fruits are oval or cylindrical in shape, resemble to date fruit, dark purple in colour, thin skinned, sweet, juicy, with a layer of light purple pulp of 0.5 cm thickness and are edible.

One seed in each fruit, not easily separable from the pulp, hard, light purple or whitish purple in colour, 1 cm x 0.25 cm, cylindrical and with a vertical suture.

Trees are shady and ornamental, so planted along roads, paths in the middle of lawn or grasslands and on marginal lands. Fruits and leaves are valued as a medicine. Seeds are also used in many medicinal and pharmaceutical preparations.

Nutritive value of 100 g pulp is : moisture 83.7 g, protein 0.7 g, fat 0.3 g, mineral matter 0.4 g, fiber 0.9 g, carbohydrates 14.0 g, calcium 15 mg, phosphorus 15 mg, iron 0.43 mg, magnesium 39 mg, sodium 26 mg, potassium 55 mg, sulphur 13 mg, sodium 26.2 mg, Vita A 48 I.U., Thiamine 0.03 mg, Riboflavin 0.01 mg, Niacin 0.02 mg, Vita C 18 mg, calorific value is 62 Kcal.

Wood is moderately hard, fairly durable for making handles of tools, parts of agricultural implements, used in buildings, etc. Good for fuel.

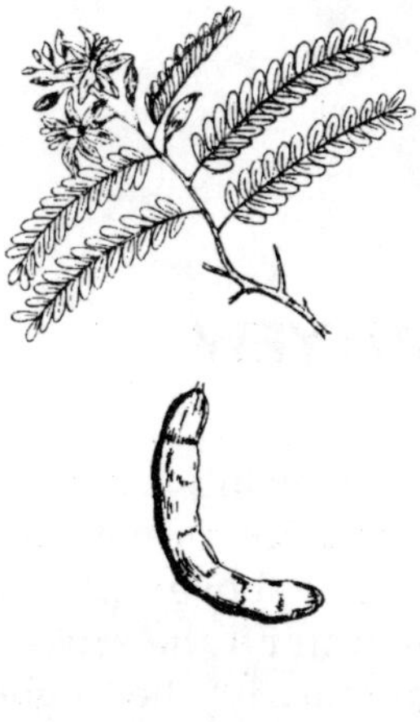

Tamarindus Indica

TAMARIND

Trees are found in the tropical region as well as in the sub-tropical region. They are even found in the drier parts, as they are able to withstand drought to some extent. They are quite common in the central part of the country. There are no planned plantations but the trees are planted along the roadsides and in gardens in the central and southern parts of India.

Botanical name of the tree is *Tamarindus indica* L. and belong to family *Caesalpiniaceae* while the vernacular name is Imli.

Trees are evergreen in nature and are large, may go as high as 18 m. Spread of the tree is almost 6 to 8 m. Bark is brownish grey and somewhat shaggy. Canopy is oval to round but with lopping it assumes uneven shape.

Leaves are compound, pinnate, leaflets 20-40, oblong, opposite, 1 to 2 cm long, green, slightly leathery and bit acidic.

Flowers are borne in summer in lax racemes that are drooping, yellowish with red streaks, and in small clusters among the leaves.

Fruits are pods, brown, which are 8-20 cm long and 2-3 cm broad, plump, slightly curved with a thin brittle shell containing a soft and fleshy brownish pulp traversed by a strong branched fibre enclosing 1-12 flattened, shining, round to oval seeds that are 1 cm across and of dark brown colour. Pulp is acidic in nature.

Trees are ornamental, avenue, shade and of medicinal value. They are mostly planted along the roadsides and in gardens. The pulp is used in many cooking preparations and seeds are eaten after roasting. Wood is used for furniture, hand-tools, charcoal, etc.

Tender leaves contain 70.5 g moisture, 5.8 g protein, 1.5 g fat, 2.2 g minerals, 1.0 g fibre, 9.4 g carbohydrates, 101 mg calcium, 140 mg phosphorus, 0.30 mg iron, Vita A 250 I.U., 0.24 mg Thiamine, 0.17 mg Riboflavin, 4.1 mg Niacin, 3 mg ascorbic acid and provides 115 Kcal energy per 100 g.

100 g of pulp has 20.9 g moisture, 3.1 g protein, 0.1 g fat, 2.9 g minerals, 5.6 g fibre, 67.4 g carbohydrates, 170 mg calcium, 100 mf phosphorus, 17.0 mg iron, Vita A 60 I.U., 0.07 mg Riboflavin, 0.7 mg Niacin, 3 mg ascorbic acid and provides 283 Kcal energy.

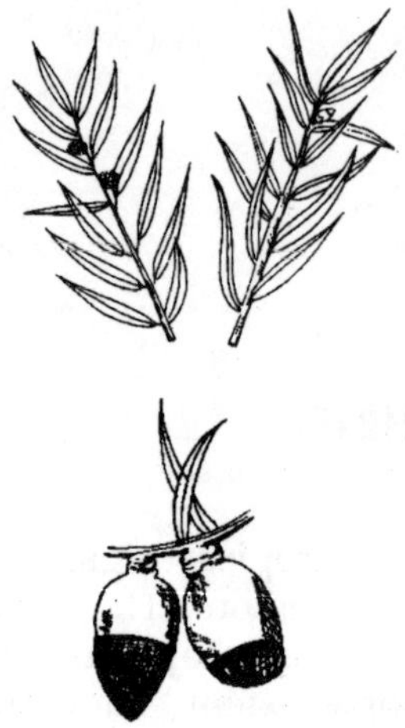

Taxus Baccata

HIMALAYAN YEW

Trees are found growing in the Himalayas between 1800 and 3500 m elevation but generally, they are best above 2200 m elevation. It is quite common in all the areas in Temperate Himalayas, particularly the higher hills and is found from Afghanistan to South-West China, Myanmar, South-East Asia.

Botanical name is *Taxus baccata* Linn. sub-sp. wallichiana and belongs to Family *Taxaceae (Coniferae).* In vernacular, it is known as Birmi.

These are evergreen and bushy in nature. It can grow to height of 15 m with reddish to dark reddish bark which is smooth in the early stages, but peels off in thin flakes with age, later becomes rough. Crown is irregular, globose and branching is low.

Leaves are flattened, linear and curved, sickle shaped; spiny tipped, leathery, 2.3 cm-5 cm long, 0.3 cm broad, borne on hairless branches.

Male and female flowers are usually on separate trees. Male flowers appear in clusters during March-May. Male cones are 0.7 cm across while female cones are bud like.

Fruits are red, fleshy, 8 mm across, often almost concealing the single green seed. Fleshy part is edible.

Seeds are olive green and highly poisonous.

Wood is burned as incense and branches are carried in processions in Kumaon region of Uttaranchal. It is also used for bow-making. Wood is durable, used for cabinet making, furniture, poles and axils of carts. Foilage contains an alkaloid, which can kill an animal if taken in excess.

Tectona Grandis

TEAK

Though it is a tree of dry Tropical region but has been introduced and planted in Uttaranchal, West Bengal, Assam, etc., where they have been found to grow successfully. Because of high value of timber, it is also being grown in the lower valleys of Shivalik range and outer Himalayas also.

Botanical name is *Tectona grandis* Linn f. which belongs to the Family *Verbenaceae.* In vernacular, the species is known as Sagwan.

It is a large deciduous tree with a long clean bole and light crown. It may grow as tall as 60 m with a good spread and less branching. Bark is greyish brown, fibrous with shallow longitudinal fissures and exfoliating in long narrow flakes.

Leaves are ovate, 50-60 cm long and 30 cm across, downy on underside. Leaves fall during summer.

Flowers are bluish-white, grow in panicles that are 30-35 cm long and appear during rainy season.

Fruits are like plume, hard, drupe, spherical, brownish, enclosed in a thick spongy covering of hairs.

Seeds are heavy and compact, 1-3, oblong.

Wood is moderately hard and is used for quality furniture, parquet floors and veneers. Wood is easy to polish and is durable.

Terminalia Arjuna

ARJUNA

Trees are found growing throughout the greater part of the country in Sub-Himalayan region that includes Madhya Pradesh, Chhatisgarh, Bihar, Maharashtra, Tamil Nadu, and valleys in the Himalayan tract, as they are successful up to 1200 m above mean sea level in the hills and valley areas. These trees are mostly seen near the watercourses, stream banks and scattered places as they love moisture near their root zone.

Botanical name of the tree is *Terminalia arjuna* W. and R. and this belongs to family *Combretaceae* while the vernacular name is Arjun, Arjan, etc.

Trees are evergreen and large, both tall and drooping but with spreading canopy that may be oval or round. Trunk is buttressed with a thick bark that is greenish white in the beginning and becomes grey in older trees but is exfoliating.

Leaves oblong or elliptic oblong, green on upper side but pale green beneath, sub-opposite, petioled and leathery to some extent.

Bloom is from March to June and flowers are sessile, pale-yellowish white, cup-shaped, small, crowded on terminal large axis, and are fragrant.

Fruit is a drupe, 2.5 to 5 cm long, ovoid or ovoid-oblong, woody, fibrous, glabrous, dark brown with 5 hard protecting wings.

Seed is bold and remains in the fruit.

Trees are good shade, landscaping and ornamental in nature. Wood is used for industrial timber, small timber, poles, fuel, etc. Leaves are edible by animals. Gum and tannin is also extracted from the trees. Bark contains arjunin and some other compounds that are used in medicines and for tanning.

Terminalia Bellirica

BELLIRIC MYROBALAN

Trees are found scattered in the sub-Himalayan tract upto 1200 m altitude in mixed deciduous forests and in moist climate where they get rainfall between 1000-3000 mm per annum. They occur almost in whole of the country excepting the dry regions of Western India.

Botanical name of the tree is *Terminalia bellirica* (Gaertn.) Roxb. and belongs to the Family *Combretaceae*. Vernacular name is Bahera.

It is a large tree often going as high as 15-20 m with a spread of about 8-10 m. Trunk is often buttressed. Bark is usually brown grey.

Leaves large, 10-25 cm long, small petiole, pointed at their tips and clustered near ends of branches.

Flowers are small, pale green to greenish white, appear during spring, i.e. March-May when the tree bears new leaves had smelling and in simple spikes.

Fruits are 2-3 cm long, ovoid, brownish and densely covered with hairs. They ripen from November to February. There is one seed in each fruit.

Bahera is basically a drug, which is a dried fruit of this tree. Fruits and leaves are used for many purposes in pharmaceutical preparations. Fruits are highly priced for their medicinal value. They are bitter in taste but used for the treatment of piles, dropsy, diarrhoea, leprosy and many other diseases. It is one of the major three constituents of Triphla, an Ayurvedic tonic preparation. Half-ripe fruit is purgative while ripe fruit has the opposite effect.

Timber is used in house construction. Being of good quality towards water resistance, it is used for making plywood and rafters, boats, etc. Bark is useful in the treatment of anaemia and leucoderma. Material for tanning leather and for dyeing of cloth is extracted from fruits.

Leaves are lopped for fodder; they contain 8.63 to 13.98 per cent crude protein and 16.73 to 18.59 per cent crude fibre.

Terminalia Chebula

CHEBULIC MYROBALAN

Trees are found growing at many places, mostly as scattered on marginal and wastelands, borders and to some extent in drier forests upto an elevation of 900 to 1500 m above mean sea level. It is found in low-lying valleys throughout the hilly areas of Himalaya, particularly from the Sutlej River eastwards. Kangra, Bilaspur and Nahan areas of Himachal Pradesh have these trees. It is also common in Jammu and Uttaranchal.

Harar or Harad is known by many other Hindi names like Har, Harra, Haritaki, etc., but Harad is most common. Botanical name is *Terminalia chebula* Retz. and this belongs to Family *Combretaceae* to which the other constituents of Triphla, Bahera belongs. Mostly it is a middle-sized tree that may become large under most suitable conditions of growth. Tree has a rounded spreading canopy/crown with short but clean trunk. Bark is dark brown which is longitudinally fissured and with woody exfoliations.

It is a deciduous tree, which remains leafless for some period. New flush of leaves appears during the spring from March to May. It may behave as evergreen under plain areas. Leaves are 10-25 cm long, ovate, acute, not crowded at ends of branches but in almost pairs. There are two small glands near the leaf-base.

Flowers are dull white in spikes at the ends of branches and they appear along with leaves in spring from March to May in North India while it may delay for a month in valley areas.

Fruit is a drupe, ellipsoid or ovoid, 2-4 cm long and 1 to 1.5 cm in diameter, has 5 ribs on its body. They start ripening from November to March depending upon the locality.

Seeds are hard nuts.

Trees are multipurpose in nature as they serve the purpose of a social forestry tree and a medicinal tree. The tree is one of the principal tannings yielding specie of commercial importance. Fruits are used for making preserve and in Triphla and the Chyavanprash. Powdered Harad is used in a number of ways as it can heal wounds and scalds or used as a gargle. Fruits are laxative in nature. Pulp of the fruit is used as a dentifrice to cure bleeding and ulceration of gums. The timber is used for making doors, posts, beams, carts and agricultural implements. Leaves of the tree provide fodder of medium quality for cattle.

Terminalia Tomentosa

LAUREL

It is one of the most common and widely distributed tree of Indian forests, which is mostly in dry regions. It becomes gregarious when grown on stiff soil near the depressions and edges of swamps. It occurs common in the sub-Himalayan tract from the River Ravi eastwards to Goalpara in Assam upto 1200 m

Tree in vernacular, i.e. Hindi is known as Sain, Asna, Saj, etc. Botanical name is *Terminalia tomentosa* W. and A. and belongs to Family *Combretaceae*.

It is a large deciduous tree with a clean bole and a full crown. It may go as high as 25 m or so. Bark is grey to black divided into oblong scales, exfoliating in thick rectangular flakes.

Leaves drop during winter and new leaves appear in May. They are sub-opposite or the uppermost alternate and elliptic, ovate or obovate-oblong, 10-20 cm x 6-10 cm, coriaceous, base often cordate, softly silky tomentose with 1-2 glands near the base of the mid-rib on the underside, margin entire or crenulate and petiole small.

Flowers are of white to dull yellow in colour, which appear in small branchlets during June-July.

Fruit is a drupe, 3.5-5.0 cm long, with 5 broad, coriaceous, horizontally veined wings, thin, and irregularly crenulate on the margins, green when immature but brown when mature.

Wood is dark brown with darker streaks, hard, strong, of variable durability and is used for building carts, railway wagons and for other purposes. It can resist moisture to some extent. Bark contains 18.7 per cent tannin and can be used as a cheap tanning material for leather. Leaves are lopped for fodder for cattle and for rearing silkworms.

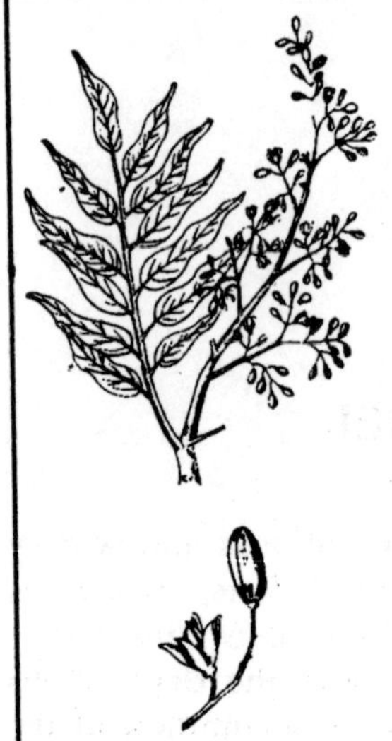

Toona Ciliata

TOON

Trees are found in the sub-Himalayan tract and valleys, particularly in the western Himalayas along the Sutlej valley. They are found in shady ravines and along streams and the altitudinal range of their occurrence is upto 1300 m in the hills under moist and semi-moist monsoon forests.

Botanical name of the tree is *Toona ciliata* M. Roem. and its synonym is *Cedrela toona* Roxb. and Family is *Meliaceae.*

Trees are deciduous, large in size and have spreading crown. Bark is dark grey, intricately cracked and exfoliating in irregular woody scales.

New leaves of dark red colour appear in early spring, i.e. February to April. Leaves are alternate, green, mid-rib and other veins quite prominent, even-pinnate, leaflets 10-20, nearly opposite or sometimes alternate, 5-7 cm and entire.

Small white and honey scented flowers appear along with new leaves during April-May.

Fruits are oblong in shape, capsular, 1 cm x 0.5 cm, ripe in May-June.

Seeds are small with membranous wings at both ends.

It is an excellent avenue tree, as the new foliage appears when almost all other deciduous trees are leafless. It is good for afforestation and plantations for development of marginal and waste lands.

Wood is of red colour but soft, shining and widely used for making furniture and handles of implements and hand-tools. Also used for manufacture of tea-boxes, building construction, etc. Branches and leaves are lopped for fodder.

Tsuga Dumosa

HIMALAYAN HEMLOCK

Trees are found in the elevation range of 2100 to 3500 m above mean sea level in the Himalayan tract from Uttaranchal to Bhutan in pure forests in humid valleys and mountain ranges or slopes.

Botanical name is *Tsuga dumosa* D. Don and the tree belongs to family *Pinaceae*. Its local name is Tunsen. It is a beautiful pyramidal evergreen tree, which may grow as tall as 40 m but generally the tree is 20 to 25 m in height.

Branches are spreading and pendulous, branchlets are hairy with leaves in two ranks.

Leaves linear, flattened, 1.5-2.5 cm x 2 cm, broad, nearly white beneath with recurved margins, glaucescent, generally opposite.

Flowers are unisexual, the males form globose catkins, the females are terminals with scales each carrying 2 ovules at the base.

Cones are small, ovoid, 1.5 cm-2.5 cm long with thin rounded scales.

Seeds are winged.

Wood is soft and timber is of little value. Logs are used as support for bridges. Cones as a fuel are in use. Tannin is contained in bark, which is used for dyeing of hides.

Ulmus Wallichiana

ELM

Trees are found throughout the Western Himalayas in Jammu-Kashmir, Himachal Pradesh and Uttaranchal between the altitudinal range of 1500-3000 m above mean sea level mostly near the moist areas and ravines.

In Hindi, the Elm tree is known as Bren, Brera, or Amari. Elm is botanically *Ulmus wallichiana* Planchon that belongs to family *Ulmaceae*.

It is a large (20-30 m tall) deciduous tree with rough grey bark. Young shoots are hairy.

Leaves are elliptic to obovate, long, pointed, double toothed. Mature leaves have rough surface, 15-20 pairs of lateral veins each ending in a large tooth, 8-10 cm long.

Flowers are 3 mm long, short stalked, green, appear in globular clusters before the emergence of leaves during spring.

Flowers are red brown, appear before the leaves, bisexual, clustered in racemes and about 2.5 cm long.

Fruit is a winged nut or samara surrounded by a wide papery wing spreading to 1.5 cm. Single seed in each nut.

Wood is used for furniture making while bark is used for making ropes out of the fibre. Leaves along with young shoots are lopped for fodder, which are quite nutritive.

Zizyphus-Jujuba

BER

Though the trees are of tropical origin but are found in the valleys and mid-hills of Western Himalayas. Trees of cultivated specie are tall and spreading while wild ones are bushes or shrubs and with more spines and smaller leaves. Trees are found almost in every part of the country.

There are two specie commonly found. *Zizyphus jujuba* Lam. and *Zizyphus mauritiana* Lamk which bear fruits of smaller size that are acidic when tender but turns sweet on maturity. They do have little pulp and are used for raising of seedling plants that are grafted with suitable scions to have good sized and sweet fruits. Commonly known as Ber in vernacular in this region.

Tree belongs to the family *Rhamnaceae* of *Angiosperm* group. Trees are generally evergreen but under unfavorable climatic conditions they behave as deciduous trees. Trees are usually 8 m tall and of 6 m spread. Canopy is round to oval. Branching is quite variable, upright to drooping but strong with good crotch angles. Bark is light brown, scaly or papery which peels off. Thorns are here and there.

Leaves vary in size, from 3 cm to 8 cm long and 1.5 cm to 6 cm wide, leathery, oblong to oval in shape, tomentose on the lower surface while upper surface is shining.

Flowers appear in September, which are greenish in colour. They are borne in short axils in large numbers.

Fruits are drupes, greenish yellow to brown in colour and round to oblong. Skin is not separable and is edible along with the pulp. Pulp is sweet and slightly scented.

Seeds are not separable from pulp, brown, hard-coated, non-endospermic, tuberculated and pointed on both ends and furrowed.

Trees and bushes are raised for fencing and for fruits. They have both therapeutic and nutritive value; leaves and fruits are used in many medicinal preparations. Leaves are used as fodder. It is a good fuel tree with hard timber of medium quality which is used for agricultural purposes.

Fruits are eaten both when mature and on drying.

Pulp (100 g) of the fruit contains 81.6 g moisture, 0.8 g protein, 0.3 g fat, 0.3 g mineral matter 17.0 g carbohydrates, 4 mg calcium, 9 mg phosphorus, 5 mg iron, 70 I.U. Vita A, 30 mg Vita B and 23 mg Vita C and Calorific value is 74 to 79 Kcal per 100 g of pulp.

INDEX

U

V

W

Y

Z